The Last Sanctuary in Aleppo

Alaa Aljaleel is an electrician turned ambulance driver
from Aleppo. Since the Syrian civil war broke out, he has
been working tirelessly to save the lives of both people
and animals, and is the founder of Ernesto's House,
a sanctuary for abandoned animals in Aleppo.

Diana Darke is the author of *My House in Damascus*
and *The Merchant of Syria*. After studying Arabic at
Oxford University, Diana Darke worked for the British
government and GCHQ, and has lived in Syria, Egypt
and with a Bedouin tribe. She is married with
two children, both born in Cairo.

Alaa Aljaleel
with Diana Darke

The Last Sanctuary
in Aleppo

A Remarkable True Story of Courage,
Survival and Hope

HEADLINE

First published in Great Britain in 2019 by
HEADLINE PUBLISHING GROUP

First published in paperback in 2019 by
HEADLINE PUBLISHING GROUP

1

Cataloguing in Publication Data is available from the British Library

ISBN 978 1 4722 6058 1

Designed and typeset by EM&EN
Printed and bound in Great Britain by Clays Ltd, Elcograf S.p.A.

Headline's policy is to use papers that are natural, renewable and recyclable
products and made from wood grown in well-managed forests and other
controlled sources. The logging and manufacturing processes are expected
to conform to the environmental regulations of the country of origin.

HEADLINE PUBLISHING GROUP
An Hachette UK Company
Carmelite House
50 Victoria Embankment
London EC4Y 0DZ

www.headline.co.uk
www.hachette.co.uk

Contents

ALEPPO

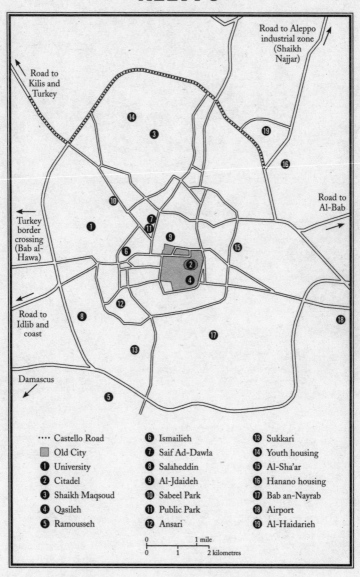

··· Castello Road
▨ Old City
❶ University
❷ Citadel
❸ Shaikh Maqsoud
❹ Qasileh
❺ Ramousseh
❻ Ismailieh
❼ Saif Ad-Dawla
❽ Salaheddin
❾ Al-Jdaideh
❿ Sabeel Park
⓫ Public Park
⓬ Ansari
⓭ Sukkari
⓮ Youth housing
⓯ Al-Sha'ar
⓰ Hanano housing
⓱ Bab an-Nayrab
⓲ Airport
⓳ Al-Haidarieh

0   1 mile
0   1   2 kilometres

Road to Aleppo
industrial zone
(Shaikh
Najjar)

Road to
Kilis and
Turkey

Turkey
border
crossing
(Bab al-
Hawa)

Road to
Al-Bab

Road to
Idlib and
coast

Damascus

Glossary

This glossary contains a selection of words mentioned in the book which may be less familiar to a Western readership. Please note that Arabic spellings can vary significantly between different sources (for example, the pipe for smoking flavoured tobacco referred to in this book as a *shisha* can also acceptably be spelt *sheesha* or known by the names *arghileh* or *hookah*). The spellings below should therefore be seen as just one version out of the many interpretations.

Abd al-Rahman/Abu Huraira – a companion of Muhammad and narrator of thousands of *hadith*

Abu Ghraib – a maximum security prison complex in Iraq, used for detentions by the US-led coalition occupying Iraq

Al-Assad, Bashar – President of Syria since 2000, following the death of father Hafez Al-Assad

Al-Assad, Hafez – Ruler of Syria, 1970–2000, succeeded by son Bashar Al-Assad

Glossary

Alawites – the sect of Shia Islam which the Assad family belong to

Al-Baghdadi – the leader of terrorist organisation ISIS

Al-Jaysh Al-Hurr – the Free Syrian Army; a faction in opposition to the Assad regime

Al-Qaeda – the militant Islamist organisation founded by Osama bin Laden

Ba'athist – a political party that promotes the creation of a united Arab state

Ben Ali, Zine El Abidine – President of Tunisia, 1987–2011

Circassian – displaced peoples from the North Caucasus

Daesh – Arabic name for ISIS

de Mistura, Staffan – Italian-Swedish diplomat, former UN Special Envoy to Syria

Dhu al-Hijja – the twelfth and final month in the Islamic calendar, during which the hajj (pilgrimage to Mecca) takes place

Dhu al-Qa'dah – the eleventh month in the Islamic calendar, one of four during which war is prohibited

Eid Al-Fitr – celebration that marks the end of Ramadan

Eidiyeh – an Eid tradition of giving monetary gifts to children

Fatiha – the opening verse of the Quran

fatwa – a special judgement on Islamic law given by a religious authority

Five Pillars of Islam – consisting of faith, prayer, charity, fasting and pilgrimage

Glossary

fool – a staple middle Eastern food, consisting primarily of
beans and chickpeas

hadith – the recorded sayings and actions of Muhammad

Halab – the Arabic name of Aleppo

haraam – forbidden by Islamic law and the Quran

iftaar – the first meal eaten at sunset during Ramadan,
breaking the daily fast

Jabhat Al-Nusra – the Syrian branch of Al-Qaeda; a jihadist
organisation in opposition to the Syrian regime

jinni – a genie or supernatural spirit

Kaaba – the shrine at the centre of Mecca's mosque

kaafir – an 'unbeliever'; someone who rejects the teachings
of Islam

Kurd – a stateless ethnic group indigenous to adjacent areas
of Turkey, Iran, Iraq and Syria

labneh – a thick yoghurt/soft cheese

Lailat Al-Qadar – the 27th night of Ramadan,
commemorating the night when God revealed the Quran
to Muhammad

Liwa Al-Tawheed – a militant Islamist group formed in 2012
from rebel groups near Aleppo

Makhlouf, Rami – cousin of Bashar al-Assad, owner of
mobile network provider Syriatel

mazout – a low quality fuel oil

minbar – a mosque's pulpit, from which imams deliver
sermons

Glossary

Mubarak, Husni – President of Egypt, 1981–2011

Muharram – the first month in the Islamic calendar, one of four during which war is prohibited

Muslim Brotherhood – a conservative Sunni Muslim group banned in 1963 by the ruling Ba'athists

National Defence Forces (NDF) – pro-regime local militias set up in 2013, armed and trained by Iran

Qaddafi, Muammar – Leader of Libya, 1969–2011

Rajab – the seventh month of the Islamic calendar, one of four during which war is prohibited

Ramadan – the ninth month of the Islamic calendar, during which fasting is observed in daylight hours

Saladin – sultan who united Egypt and Syria, of Kurdish ethnicity, died 1193 in Damascus

Seljuk – an eleventh-century Turko-Persian empire

servees – a minibus shared taxi

shabiha – 'ghosts', armed militia employed by the Assad regime, mostly Alawite

shaikh – an Islamic elder, scholar or leader

Shi'a – one of the two major denominations of Islam; regard Ali, cousin of Muhammad, as his rightful successor

shisha – water pipe for smoking flavoured tobacco. Also known as *arghileh* or *hookah*

Sufi – Muslim mystic

Sunni – one of the two major denominations of Islam; recognise Abu Bakr as Muhammad's rightful successor

Glossary

Turcoman – Syrian citizens of Turkish origin

waasta – having connections or influence; loosely translates into 'nepotism'

za'atar – a herbal mix

Zakat Al-Fitr – the charity of the breaking of the fast, given during Ramadan

Prologue

The Castello Road was 'the most dangerous road in the world'. That's what all the news channels were calling it, during the battle for Aleppo. It was at the very frontline of the hostilities, and for four years, from 2012 until 2016, it was also my workplace. I would wait in my ambulance, parked beside the old 'Elegance' biscuit factory, the one that made the wafers we all loved as children, long before the war, watching the road. I would sit there, sometimes for hours, waiting for the bombs to arrive and for my work to begin.

My pocket as I sat there would be full of luncheon meat scraps, and I'd often have a cat perched on the dashboard beside me. Some of the cats from my sanctuary would follow me around wherever I went, I think because they found it comforting. But in all honesty, it was often the other way round. The final very intense period of bombing, in 2016, was close to my home and to the cat sanctuary I'd created, in Hanano, the very north-eastern corner of Aleppo. The Syrian regime's army was in west Aleppo, the opposition fighters were in east Aleppo, and I would park my ambulance just east of east Aleppo. It meant I could reach the bombed areas quickly, within minutes.

As the only route in and out of east Aleppo, the Castello Road was targeted from all directions. Everything had to come in and out via that road: all our food, fuel and medicines, all the essentials of life. It snaked out in a big loop, heading north from the city centre near Aleppo University, then curved east past the Kurdish enclave of Shaikh Maqsoud and the Youth Housing District, until it reached the Aleppo countryside. Those first two or three kilometres were the most dangerous stretch. Anyone could hit you there – the regime, the Russians, the Kurds or just random thieves, who might claim to be from any faction. All sides could see every vehicle going in or out.

The Syrian regime was shelling the Castello Road with artillery from the west, while their Russian allies in fighter jets were dropping bombs from above in support. They wanted to put the road out of action entirely, to block it and control it, so that they could put us under siege in east Aleppo and force the rebels who'd retreated to that area of the city to surrender.

The Kurds, meanwhile, had snipers who would shoot at any civilians brave enough to flee along this deadly stretch, because they assumed they must be the families of the rebel Free Syrian Army. The regime had done a deal with the Kurds, allowing them to stay in Aleppo to defend their enclave as long as they also helped fight the rebels. The regime and the Kurds considered all civilians, like me, who lived in east Aleppo, to be terrorists, so we were all targeted indiscriminately.

As for the thieves, they were just opportunists who could be from any faction or none; they were the sort of mercenary, greedy people who appear in any war. They had realized that a lot of people trying to escape Aleppo would be carrying all their valuables with them – gold, jewellery, cash – so if the bombs and bullets didn't get you, the thieves probably would. They shot people in order to steal their valuables.

★

The last of the many casualties I carried from the Castello Road, before the regime entered the area and closed off Aleppo completely, was a man who worked in Turkey and was travelling back for the Eid holiday after Ramadan. Eid is our most holy time, and the regime had supposedly declared this period as a truce. But the next day they broke it. It had all been a trick to catch people off their guard during the holidays. The siege proper began on the second day of Eid, blocking the road in and out of Aleppo once and for all.

For that poor man we carried from the Castello Road, however, we were too late to save his life. He was already dead by the time we reached him, but we wanted to retrieve his body and luggage for his family's sake. The road then fell under bombardment again, so I told everyone to get into the car and we drove quickly back to east Aleppo. I'll never forget how, when we opened his bag, we found it was full of gifts and toys. They were presents he'd bought for his kids to celebrate Eid. He'd even bought them new clothes; they still had their labels on.

That rescue was the last time I drove the Castello Road, and I was the last person to leave it. Five minutes later, the army had completely closed off our part of the city. Our home was now surrounded.

1: Growing up in Aleppo

My favourite dish when I was young, and I'm still fond of it now, is cooked rice mixed with yogurt. My mother used to tell a story about me and this food, from when I was only four years old and we were living in a small courtyard house in the Old City of Aleppo, a story which maybe shows that I loved all animals, not just cats, right from the very beginning. As she told it, one day, on a bright summer morning, I took my bowl of rice and yogurt down to the cellar. Most old Aleppo houses had cellars where the food was stored, and that morning the door had been left open. When she noticed I'd disappeared, she came looking for me and found me there, sitting under the stairs with my bowl. But in my lap was a shiny snake, green and yellow, with black lines, about one and a half metres long, glistening in the sunlight . . . I was eating with my right hand and holding its head with my left hand, putting its mouth into the bowl of rice and yogurt, as if inviting it to eat.

The way my mother recounted it, she was screaming inside, but she said nothing, because she didn't want to

5

startle the snake and provoke it. She didn't panic. She just turned slowly around and, once she was out of the cellar, she rushed out into the street and called out to all the neighbours. Everybody came running to help, but by then the snake had disappeared. They searched and found the hole where the snake could have slipped away. At that time it was well known that these old buildings often had snakes, but my parents didn't want to leave it there, so they called in some people who were experts in reptiles. My mother described the snake to them and they said: 'Don't worry, this kind of snake doesn't attack people. It's harmless and will have lived in the house a long time. You can feed it and it'll only hurt you if you threaten it, so you don't need to worry about your son going into the cellar. There's nothing to be afraid of.' Somehow that story has stayed with me, like a talisman of sorts, and all my life I've been fortunate to have faced many dangers without feeling afraid, just as when I befriended the snake as a small boy.

*

I have always been proud to have been born and raised in Aleppo, which is such an ancient and important city. In Arabic we call it 'Halab', which means 'milk'. Some people say this is because of the famous white Aleppo stone, which is similar to the colour of milk, but a local tradition suggests it comes from the legend that the Prophet Abraham stopped in Aleppo on his way south and milked a cow to feed the poor. This is why the city's nickname is 'Al-Shahba', which is a type of local black-and-white cow, and souvenir shops sell little figures of cows in tribute. All of us in Aleppo had a real sense of the city's rich traditions, because we could see history everywhere around us: the old centre was full of fine public buildings, such as mosques, bath-houses, churches and cathedrals, all built from the beautiful white limestone.

But even as children we understood that the reason for all this wealth was the souks. We used to get lost in the maze of alleyways, more than twelve kilometres long. People would tell us they were the biggest covered souks anywhere in the world, and in the summer they were wonderfully cool, because of the stone arched ceilings and ventilation holes. At midday, when the sun was directly overhead, shafts of light would come straight down through these holes and make magic squares that we loved to dance in and out of on the flagstones. Then, as the sun moved across the sky, the beams would come in at different angles, sometimes lighting up the fabulous colours of the textiles – gorgeous reds, greens and yellows, spread out in front of the shops – and sometimes illuminating the aromatic herbs and spices neatly arranged in sacks. Each trade had its own area according to what it sold, so you had, for example, the cloth market, the soap market, the spice market and the saddlers' market, where all the traders sold pretty much the same thing. People used to joke that, if you were blind, you could still find your way around the souks, just by following the smells of what was for sale. The streets of the souks were always clean, because a special workers union swept them and collected the rubbish every day. In the old days, that rubbish was then sold to the bathhouses in the souk, to be burnt in their furnaces to heat the water. It was a clever kind of early recycling.

Although the souks were always busy, full of local people buying their daily shopping and a few tourists buying souvenirs, the shopkeepers always had time to socialize with their customers, inviting them in to sip tea or to smoke a shisha. The skill of Aleppo's merchants and traders was respected and admired all across the Middle East. 'What was sold in the souks of Cairo in a month, was sold in Aleppo in a day!' ran the local saying.

Aleppo had been the nerve centre of the Syrian economy for centuries. It was at the beginning of the Silk Road, halfway between the Mediterranean and the Euphrates River in Mesopotamia, and that's why the souks were so famous and so big. More people used to live in Aleppo than in the capital, Damascus, five hours' drive away to the south, because of all the businesses that set themselves up here, not just in the Old City, but also all the modern factories beyond the ring-road. Those factories made all the things that Aleppo was famous for – clothing and textiles, spices, laurel soap, copper, leather, gold and precious stones, rugs and carpets.

Growing up in Aleppo

The area of the Old City where I was born, on 1st January 1975, was called Asileh – it was a residential quarter just inside the walls, close to the southern gate. This is where I grew up. If you look for it on a map, you'll find it's written Al-Qasileh because, when we Syrians speak, we usually drop this 'q' sound. Many well-known, prosperous Aleppo families used to live in that neighbourhood, in beautiful grand courtyard houses. But then, from about the 1940s onwards, these old houses went out of fashion and the rich people left to live in modern suburbs instead. After they left, it became a much more modest residential area, a bit neglected, with many of the houses divided between poorer tenants or even used as warehouses for the nearby souks. The really rich people used to have three courtyards all to themselves, but today people live in far more cramped conditions.

★

My family loved living in the Old City, but my father didn't like the thought of the snake living with us in the cellar. He didn't want to take the risk. Two months later he sold the house (without telling the buyer about the resident snake), and we moved away from the Old City and away from these kinds of old buildings, where snakes might lurk in the shadows.

We proceeded to move house three times during my childhood, always to other districts in Aleppo. From Asileh in the Old City we moved to Isma'iliyeh, and a bigger, more beautiful house, probably the most beautiful place we called home during my youth – me, my parents and my sister Najla. Al-Isma'iliyeh is a residential district in the west of the city centre that was developed between the 1940s and 50s. Most of the families there used to be Jewish, before the Jews left Syria. About 7 per cent of the population was Jewish in those days. They'd come to Syria originally as refugees from Spain, centuries ago, escaping the Spanish Inquisition, but they faced lots of difficulties and hostility after the state of Israel was created in 1948. When they left, they were forced to give their property to the government. It must have been very hard for them.

It was in this house in Isma'iliyeh that I remember my first special cat. My father arrived home one day, when I was about five years old, and said: 'I've got a surprise for you and Najla.' He put down a fluffy white ball of fur on the floor in front of us. 'I've brought her from your granddad's house.' Our grandparents' cat, Baysalan, used to reject her young very early, so her kittens always got given away to various uncles, aunts and other relations, so that every family got one. We called the tiny kitten 'Lulu', which means 'pearl' in Arabic, because she was white like a pearl.

My sister Najla was a year older than me. We were so happy to have Lulu. We fought a lot about which of us would take care of her, but most of the time we agreed and looked after her together. She was like a doll that each of us longed to have to ourselves. So Lulu would spend one day in my room and the next in Najla's room. We took it in turns to be her mother, looking after her in every way. We used to wash her, give her food, comb her fur, make special clothes for her and play with her all the time, dangling a ball of wool for her to chase. Lulu clearly liked us both, but to be honest, she liked my sister more, maybe because Najla knew better than I did how to make things that cats like. This made me very envious of my sister, and so I tried hard to make Lulu like me more. I always wanted her to choose me and come and sit in my lap. But all my efforts were in vain, and she definitely liked Najla the best.

My grandparents on my father's side, the ones who had Baysalan, Lulu's mother, were very concerned with the welfare of cats, so my sister Najla and I learned our love of cats from them. All of us in the family got the habit from them, and it's an unusual habit to have in this part of the world, because many Arabs don't like cats, or any animals for that matter. And yet, in Islam, the life of a cat is considered to be precious, so it must just be ignorance and lack of education that makes people in Arab countries dislike animals and treat them badly. Cats aren't specifically mentioned in the Quran, but there are plenty of times when cats appear in the Hadith sayings of the Prophet Muhammad. He's known to have respected cats, and he even threatened hell-fire to a woman who tortured her cats. We also know he must have had a cat at home, as a pet in his house, because his young wife A'isha, after his death, is recorded as saying: 'Even the cat has left me alone.'

My grandfather had a big heart and was a very kind man, and he was always feeding strays. He taught me a Turkish proverb that says: 'Those who love cats have a strong faith'. He also told me a very nice story about cats and an Islamic mystic – we call them 'Sufi' in Arabic. This Sufi lived and died in the tenth century, but he appeared in a dream to a modern man living in the twentieth century. In the man's dream, the Sufi asked God which of his many pious acts had gained him the most forgiveness, and gave a long list of his good deeds, such as his prayers, his fasting and his almsgiving. But God told him: 'No, not for all these have I forgiven you, but for that cold winter's night when you saw a kitten shivering against a wall and put it under your fur coat'.

My grandfather made his living from the windmill he owned, five kilometres outside Aleppo in an area called Fifeen, past the central prison. He used to walk there every day to grind the barley for the villagers in all the surrounding villages, and then he would walk back again at the end of the day. I don't remember him that well, sadly, because I was only seven when he died, but when I think of him now, I remember that proverb and that story. My father told us lots of stories about him, which helps him live on in our minds.

There was one, for example, about how my grandfather climbed down inside a very deep pit of water, a well of some kind, because a cat had fallen down it. He managed to rescue the cat, thankfully, even though the pit was so narrow he could easily have got stuck inside too. Once he was at the bottom, he tied a rope round the cat, then he got people to pull the cat to safety before getting out of the pit himself. Sometimes he used to bring wounded cats in from the street and take care of them and treat their injuries. He often got hurt doing this, because some of the cats were very fierce and would bite and scratch him if they'd been wounded or had had an accident and were trying to defend themselves. They didn't understand that he was trying to help them, and it could well have been unkind people who hurt them in the first place, which made them think people were their enemies. My grandfather suffered lots of injuries from these wounded cats, but it didn't stop him looking after them.

My grandparents on my mother's side, meanwhile, made their living from their clothes shop in the old souk of Aleppo. My mother's family name was Al-Jaser, and the Al-Jasers owned a lot of shops in the Old City back then. They weren't nearly so keen on animals, but we used to visit their house a lot, and, inspired by my paternal grandfather, encourage them to feed the cats. In the summer holidays, we used to stay for about a month, so we'd bring stray cats home with us and play with them in the garden. In the end, we got my mother's parents into the habit of caring for and adopting strays as well.

★

I was sent to kindergarten when I was four, but I don't remember much about it except the bus driver, Abu Saleh, who used to give us sweets to eat every day on the bus. Then, when I was seven, I moved from my kindergarten to a primary school in Aleppo, a place called Saqar Quraysh. I made lots of new friends there and would tell them all about my cat Lulu. Of course, I couldn't take her to school with me, but we had lots of happy trips and school outings, which were always fun. Even though I was never the best in the class at studying, I have nice memories of my school days there. My academic level was just average, I'm afraid, but all the teachers commented on how charismatic I was. Our school was mixed, boys and girls together, like all primary schools in Syria, and most of my friends at that time were girls. I always respected girls and treated them well. That was due to my sister Najla, who had always looked after me and taken good care of me, instilling in me a regard for girls generally. Najla even used to pack my bag for me, make my food if I was hungry, and make me juice to drink when I was doing my homework and much more. She was always so sweet to me, so I liked girls because of her.

Lulu the white cat remained with us until I was fifteen years old, and often followed us wherever we went. She was able to recognize her name and would come running whenever we called her. During the ten years she spent with us, we often tried to bring other cats to live with us too, but she always fought with them and refused to accept any other cat in the house, with the exception of one that stayed with us for about eighteen months.

Over the course of my childhood, I got to know a few other cats, but Lulu was always number one. Most of the others were strays, so never came into our home; they just came for food and then left again, and we could never make them stay. I can remember three cats I fed like this, and by the time I was eleven, I even used to teach my friends about cats and explain to them how to look after them, to the extent that I managed to convince two of my friends to have cats in their own homes.

Towards the end of her life, Lulu began to look sick and grew very thin. Najla and I couldn't understand why she looked so tired. She was ill at home for about three weeks, and then she just disappeared. She used to go out of the house through a window, and return the same way, but this time she didn't return. We were very upset, and my father tried to explain to us what happened. He knew everything about cats and their behaviour from his own father and told us that when a cat knows it's going to die, it leaves and dies far away, so that it doesn't make its owner sad. After all the years of experience I've now had with my own cats, I know that what my father told me is true, but when I was young, it came as a shock. I too believe a cat knows you'll be sad if it dies in front of you. It knows you've been taking care of it for a long time and that you have loved it, so it goes away to die silently and make you think maybe it just ran away.

After my father gently broke the news to me, I fell ill myself for a week. I was so sad about losing Lulu that I couldn't even go to school. I prayed to God over and over that she might return, as my father had left me a glimmer of hope. He'd said: 'She may return. Maybe she isn't dead? But it may take two or three months before she returns.' I think he told us this to help us adjust to the idea, to calm us down and make it easier for us. He was trying to stop us thinking about Lulu all the time, and told us we had to be patient, and that we might get another cat soon. Lulu was so very precious to me, because she was the first ever cat in my life. She never did return.

*

As well as learning about cats from my father, I also learned a lot about his job. He was a fireman. He's sixty-six and retired now, and he still lives in Aleppo. He used to work for Sadcop, the state-owned fuel company that also provides petrol coupons (Syrians used to be given the coupons to control and ration fuel buying). I always wanted to be a fireman just like him and felt that rescuing people was the best job ever. Looking after cats was always my hobby as a child, but my big ambition was to help my father in his job of rescuing people and fire fighting. Once, I remember, my father was called to put out a big fire in Aleppo, and I thought I too could try to help save people in some way, so I hid in the truck to make sure I could go with him to watch what he did. He was very surprised when he found me, but he wasn't angry. He even let me watch. After that, I often used to go with him to his workplace in Ramouseh on the outskirts of Aleppo, especially on Fridays, the weekly holiday when there was no school. There was a swimming pool out there and over a hundred local cats, all of which he'd care for.

*

The most beautiful memories I have from my primary school years are from when I was about eleven, in the fifth grade. I was with a group of friends, boys and girls, and we were always looking for some cats to play with. After school, or early in the morning before school, we used to feed local cats our sandwiches. Most of the time the cats didn't want them, especially if they were just tomato paste sandwiches or were seasoned with *za'atar*, which is a kind of herbal mix based on thyme, but sometimes we might have a piece of luncheon meat to give them. Cats really need meat; they are 100% carnivores, unlike dogs, which have stomachs more like humans and can eat everything. Midhat was my best friend at the time and we both loved cats. He had learned how to take care of cats from me, but his family wouldn't allow him to bring them home, so he used to get permission from his parents to come to study with me at home, and then he could play with my cat Lulu.

One day, Midhat and I happened to find a cat that had given birth at the entrance to a building, so we took her to an old derelict house and garden where no one was living. We found a cardboard box and arranged for her to sleep in it with her four kittens. Of course, I couldn't take her home, because we already had Lulu, and Midhat couldn't take her either, since his parents wouldn't allow him to have a cat. Even so, we made a plan. Every morning before school and every afternoon after school, we visited her, bringing food. We gave her the leftovers from our own homes, things like rice, bulgur wheat and beans. My father had told me that a cat in this sort of situation would probably eat everything and not be so fussy, but he was happy that Midhat and I were looking after her, and even gave us money to buy milk. We kept her clean, and tidied all around the cardboard box, and brought her milk and food every day. We even decorated the garden and the place where she slept with all sorts of bits and pieces we found here and there, colourful things like old toys and other bric-a-brac.

She stayed in the derelict house with her kittens for about four months in total. Her babies were very active, playing and jumping around, but we didn't stay long with them when we visited, just around 20 minutes, because we didn't want to make our parents worry about where we were. We had so much fun, playing with them as they were growing up. Some of our other friends also came with us sometimes to play with them too, at our invitation, but after about six months, we turned up one day to find they were all gone. The kittens were fully weaned and had grown up, leaving their mother free to go her own way too. After that, we glimpsed them occasionally, but then hardly saw them at all. We saw other cats from time to time in the area and often wondered if they were the same ones or not. We were sad, of course, but it had been a beautiful time while we had been looking after them all, and the most important thing was that we did our best to help this cat and her kittens.

*

My father sold the house in Isma'iliyeh when I was twelve and bought another house in Saif al-Dawla, in western Aleppo, a simple residential area in the south-west part of the city that grew up originally in the 1960s and 70s. To begin with, all the houses had gardens full of fruit trees – orange, apple and apricot mainly. I remember how naughty I was then, because I used to climb the trees with my friends and we'd mess about stealing the fruit from other people's gardens. We'd throw the apricots down to one of our friends below, who would hold out his long robe to catch them. The owners used to chase us with sticks and call us 'locusts'. Sometimes they almost got us, but we always managed to escape. A few years after we moved there, a big market opened in Saif Al-Dawla, and a lot of the gardens were sold. The land was used to build shops instead. After that it became a very crowded area full of small stores and street sellers.

★

When I was thirteen, I moved on to a secondary school in the west of the city. The school was called Al-Ameen. I made lots of new friends there, but all of them were boys, because secondary schools in Syria are not mixed like the primary schools are. My father bought me a bicycle as a reward for getting through primary school successfully and that bicycle became the great joy of my life. I loved it and cycled to school on it every day, even though it took less than five minutes. At the end of every year in Syrian schools there's an exam that you have to pass in order to continue to the next year. I stayed three years at Al-Ameen, successfully moving on to the next year each time, until the final year, when I failed. I repeated the year and then, thankfully, succeeded in getting my Intermediate Certificate at the age of seventeen. After that, I left school and started to work as an electrician.

Despite all my happy childhood memories, there are also some memories that make me sad. My father married twice. First to my mother, who was also Najla's mother, then to my stepmother. Together, my father and stepmother had six more children, so I gained three half-brothers and three half-sisters. Najla and I were never close to them, though, and after Najla herself got married, I left my father's house and went to live with my grandparents on my mother's side. My stepmother didn't like me, or Najla, so once Najla left home to move in with her new husband, I felt I should become independent and live separately from my father and his new family.

Today I live far away from my father and his new family. They all live in western Aleppo, in the areas under the control of the Assad regime – the family who've ruled Syria since 1970 – while I live in an area controlled by the rebel opposition. Where we all live now is just an accident of geography, though. It's nothing to do with politics or the war. And yet we haven't got on well together for a long time, not because we hate each other, but because they have their way of thinking and I have mine. My sister Najla now has three children of her own, two sons and a daughter. She lives with her family in the regime-held areas of Aleppo too and still visits me from time to time. She's very happy with her husband and her children and that makes me feel very happy for her too.

Tragically, my mother passed away three years ago in Turkey, after taking the wrong medicine by mistake. She was given an analgesic injection as a painkiller, but she had taken some other drugs beforehand that she didn't realize would react badly with the injection. She developed a blood clot and died. She was only fifty-seven.

I miss her very much, but, in a way, I was able to accept the news of her death better, because by then I'd seen so many other victims – men, women and children – due to the war. The shock of her death was not as bad as it might have been, because of that. My mother was very precious to me, however, and her death helped me to empathize with all the other people who've lost loved ones in the war. It made me realize all victims are precious to someone. Before the war I'd been frightened of losing my mother, but after the war began, and after seeing so many other deaths, the death of my mother was easier to bear. I felt sad, of course, but I believe that we have to accept the truth of losing loved ones. We have to be patient and bear it. In fact, after her death, I was even more motivated to help other people, to do good things on her behalf, such as distributing food to poor people, all in my mother's name. I asked those people I helped to pray to God for my mother, and to say the Fatiha, the opening verse of the Quran. I wanted to do even more to help others so that my mother could rest in peace.

2: A New Mission

Like most Syrian children, I started work very young. I liked working very much – in fact, I've never stopped working. As a result, I was virtually independent from my early teens onwards and had many adventures. During the 1980s, we were under an economic blockade from most European and Arab countries, so I used to go to nearby Lebanon to buy foodstuffs and then sell them on in Syria. That was in about 1988 and 1989, when I was thirteen and fourteen years old and still at school. I would go to an area called 'Areeda, which is the coastal border crossing between Syria and Lebanon on the main north–south highway between Tartous and Tripoli. There was a shortage of most things in Syria then, so, as well as food, I would bring back clothes, household goods and toys. I made good money this way, which I used to help my family and my friends. I loved buying and selling toys most of all, and I'd regularly give toys for free to my friends and neighbours, and to my brothers and sisters. I carried on working in the toy business for more than ten years in total.

My mother always prayed for me and asked God to help me with my work. 'May the dust turn to gold in your hands, Alaa', she used to say to me. And thanks to my mother and her prayers, God did indeed help me in my business. It made her very happy to see me working and having a good income while I was still so young. Both my parents were a big support to me, and my mother even gave me her savings to get me started in my toy business. I also worked in several places in various jobs, doing whatever work I could, and gradually earned enough money to no longer need financial support from my parents.

In Syria most children learn a trade or skill of some sort in their summer holidays. This is to make sure they can always find work, in case they fail in their studies or can't get a job with their school diploma. A typical holiday job, for example, for poorer boys, was to sell sweets on the streets or in the parks, to learn how to be tough and independent and to make a bit of money. Sometimes boys would be sent across the border into Lebanon every day over the summer to work as labourers there. Richer families sent their sons to the souks to learn how to buy and sell, especially those who lived in Aleppo and Damascus. Most of their fathers were merchants anyway, and they wanted their sons to learn how to become merchants too. Girls didn't have to do this. In fact, they weren't allowed to work outside the home, even if they wanted to. Their role was to stay at home and help their mothers with the cooking and the housework. Syrian society has always been very traditional in this way – 'the kitchen for women, the food for men' was the attitude – though this is starting to change now, because of the war, just as it did in Europe because of your wars and the changes they brought to the way people lived and worked.

When I was thirteen, I chose electrical work as my trade. I decided to become an electrician, because, as a child, I had liked coloured lights a lot and had put them everywhere in the house. I had a toy plane and had made a bar of coloured lights for that too. So, every summer after school, I practised with an electrician and he trained me like an apprentice for three years, starting from when I was fourteen. I even learnt from him how to assemble electronic boards for industrial machines. It was like a hobby for me.

I also learnt to drive at that time, when I was about sixteen, by watching my uncle. He had just invested in a fourteen-seater minibus taxi – the ones we call *servees* in Arabic – which he rented for ten years. Minibuses were new in Syria at that time, and Far Eastern makes, such as Mazda and Hyundai, started being imported by a company called Al-Rasi in Aleppo. The deal was that you rented the minibus for ten years, paying the company a daily rent of about 1,000 Syrian pounds (about US$20 at that time), and after that, they sent it off to the duty-free market to be sold, if it was still driveable by then. We used to make good money, around 5,000 Syrian pounds (US$100) a day, and I went everywhere with him in it. We'd go and collect people arriving from Damascus at the train station in Aleppo and drive them to places like Qamishli in the north and Deir Ez-Zour in the east, where there wasn't any train service. We worked day and night and even slept in the minibus.

Sometimes a cat would come with us on these trips around Syria. One special cat in particular liked being driven around at speed and would sit up front with us on the dashboard. I'd found him as a stray and noticed how quick he was in his movements. He was especially fast when he was running to get food, a bit like me, so I called him 'Al-Zeibaq', which means 'Mercury' in Arabic, like the Roman messenger god, the god of speed. Everyone in the neighbourhood knew, if food went missing, it was because Mercury had got there first. All the passengers on these minibus trips liked him, even though he was always thieving. Whenever we stopped to pick up snacks along the way, he always got something.

His name had another significance too, because, in the tales of *One Thousand and One Nights*, there's a very special character called Al-Zeibaq who defies authority and fights corruption. State corruption was a fact of life in Syria in those days and, of course, it still is. The Syrian public sector works through a system called *waasta* in Arabic, which mean 'connections' or 'contacts'. As a child, the whole system of *waasta* didn't make much of an impression on me, but once I was an adult, I saw it everywhere. For example, getting a driving licence in Syria was a big dream for every Syrian back in the 1980s and 90s. Obtaining one required a big *waasta* inside the government system, so was out of reach for most people. With *waasta*, most things were possible. Without it, you could wait for ever and get nothing.

I didn't have *waasta*, so, like lots of Syrians, I didn't take my driving test until I was over thirty, because they were more lenient on people by then. Back in the 1980s and 90s, there was no such thing as the traffic police, so people didn't worry about being checked and, to be honest, unless you had *waasta*, you'd have failed no matter how good your driving was. But by the 2000s, it was easy, because there were private driving schools where you could guarantee passing just by paying the standard 10,000 Syrian pounds (US$200) beforehand. The driving school took the money as commission, and then distributed it around the staff to supplement their salaries. I still chuckle every time I remember my driving test. I'd been driving for seventeen years by this point, but the examiner made me get out of the car before I'd even put my foot on the clutch. I was afraid he'd failed me because he wanted more money, but instead he just signed a paper to say I'd passed. 'I can tell you know how to drive,' he said, 'just from the way you got into the car and prepared to drive off. I realized you'd already been driving a long time, so there was no need to do the test.' He was right. I've always been a good driver, though I have to say road safety in Syria was never exactly a priority and no one wore a seat belt.

It was all a bit of a joke, just a corrupt money-making exercise, but it stopped being funny the day before I was supposed to collect my licence from the Traffic Department, when I was stopped at 11 o'clock at night in modern central Aleppo district by the police. Because I couldn't show my licence, the police put me in jail for seven days. On top of that, I had to pay a fine of 100,000 Syrian pounds (US$2,000) to get out.

★

Once I'd finished my education, aged eighteen, I worked independently for a year and a half in Beirut as an electrician, but then I was called up to do my compulsory military service for two years. I don't like to remember my time in military service. It was two and half years of hell. I served in the city of Suweida, in the south of Syria, in the Fifth Military Division, and in the Engineering Battalion, number 127, in Deraa, a city in the extreme south-west, a long way from Aleppo. (Deraa was the city where the Syrian Revolution later began, as it happens, in 2011, sixteen years later.) I was put in the mines subdivision. There's no choice for ordinary people, those without connections – you go where you are sent.

During my first few weeks of training we had a commanding officer who was from Aleppo. It was my first time continuously away from home and from my mother and I told the commanding officer that she was missing me a lot. He sympathized with me and with my mother, so he sent me to Aleppo – at the opposite end of the country from Deraa – for 48 hours' leave. Usually we only got 24 hours' leave, but he was kind and gave me special permission to take double that. When I came back, I brought him a present from the Aleppo countryside to thank him and left it on his desk. It was a two-kilogramme bag of *za'atar* – the special herbal mix we use a lot to flavour our food in Syria. We were always told it helped keep our bodies strong and our minds alert. He was horrified when he saw the present. He called the guard and instructed him to arrest me and put me straight in prison. I was put in prison for six hours, from 10 p.m. until 4 a.m. He didn't insult me or hit me, but he had to show the guards that he wasn't accepting a bribe from me by taking the bag of *za'atar*. After I was released, he said to me, when we were out of earshot of the guards: 'I don't need what you brought me. I know you just wanted to thank me, but people won't understand. They'll just think you bribed me to send you on leave. I sympathize with your mother's situation, so you don't need to pay me with *za'atar* or Aleppo soap or whatever else for that.' I apologized and took the bag of *za'atar* back. Can you imagine how much he protected me? I'll never forget him.

After completing this first training period, it's normal to be sent to a field battalion. But, fortunately for me, this commanding officer was able to keep me busy for four months fixing the electricity in their centre in Bosra Al-Harir, a town near Deraa. They had a new building there, so I did all the electrical work. I worked hard and did a good job. My uniform was always clean and I used to spend a lot of my savings – the money I'd earned and saved, about 50,000 Syrian pounds (around US$1000), from my electrician's work in Beirut and toy business before my military service – to buy extra food for myself and my friends. Some of the training officers told the commander of the Engineering Battalion about me, so he asked for me to be sent to them. My friend the Aleppo commanding officer told me he couldn't keep me away from the Engineering Battalion any longer, because all the electrical work at their centre was finished now. 'If I keep you any longer,' he said, 'I might be punished, because it's my responsibility to follow orders, so you must go. May God protect you.'

So I was transferred to the Engineering Battalion. These days I can laugh about what happened next, but it wasn't funny at the time. In fact, it was a living nightmare, especially for someone like me, who had never been keen on exercise and sport. In the Syrian army, every day starts with cross-country running, a distance of about eight kilometres. At 6am, on an empty stomach, we were loaded up into trucks – about 260 of us, all young soldiers doing their military service – and driven to a spot the required distance away from our battalion. Then we had to run those eight kilometres back to the battalion location in order to get our breakfast. To be fed was our reward. The food was terrible, but we were so hungry we would've eaten anything. The idea was to make us run for about forty-five minutes, and when we made it back to the camp, we had to run up to the Syrian flag, salute it and sing the national anthem. Only then were we allowed to go and have breakfast in the soldiers' mess, by which time it would usually be around 7am.

I was no winged mercury, and my running was slow and painful. So I devised a trick. Soon after the truck set off from camp, I'd jump off where there was a bit of ground cover and hang around until I saw the others running back. Then I'd join them right at the end and run back into base. It worked fine for a while, but then someone snitched on me.

One day when I jumped off the truck, the camp commandant suddenly appeared from behind a small hut close to the camp and yelled at me: 'I've caught you now!' I tried to make excuses: 'Sir, I got tired. I can't run because my knees hurt me.' He shouted back: 'But you don't worry that you might break your leg when you jump off the truck like that? From now on you'll run in front of me or with me!'

This particular camp commandant was fanatical about exercise and his battalion was known as the 'Torture Corps'. If they wanted to punish someone, they'd send him to this commandant, because they knew he gave his soldiers a really hard time. Sport for him was sacred, and I mean really strenuous sport, not easy sport. It was so tough. Physical exercise for him went beyond anything reasonable. Even after we'd been fed our basic dinner in the mess, he'd make us go out for a long march, another eight kilometres, in our full field uniforms, wearing our gas masks. We had to set off carrying our rifles, a bottle of water and an empty bag. Then we had to fill our bags with stones and carry them back to the camp. This was the special job of the Engineering Battalion, because other battalions would come to us to collect these stones and take them off to use as defence walls and to build gun emplacements. It was very tiring and we didn't get to rest and go to sleep until very late, always after midnight, usually around 2 a.m.

So this commandant made me do sport with him every day, very tough sport and lots of exercise. He completely exhausted me, until one day, when he was making me run around with a football, I had a very painful accident and hurt my leg badly. I was sent to the hospital in Deraa city, but they didn't have the right kind of surgeon there who could operate on my knee, so they transferred me to the Tishreen Military Hospital in Damascus, which specializes in war injuries. After my operation, I was given long convalescence leave for fourteen months, as that's how severe my injury had been. I was determined not to go back to my torturer, so I managed to pay someone to keep getting my leave extended and, eventually, I escaped all of the final months of my military service by remaining on convalescence leave.

A New Mission

The commandant was furious that I never returned. He wanted to punish me more, but I had finished my military service legally and was demobilized in 1997.

★

Everyone in Syria knows this time spent in military service is formative, especially since they take you into the army when you've only just turned eighteen. But what I learnt from my service is that, above all, we were not serving our country. When I was still in the Engineering Battalion, suffering under the sports-obsessed commandant, I wrote a report about this for the military security. But I was naïve to do so, as I suffered even more because of writing that report. There was a lot of humiliation in the military – people were constantly insulted. The officers used to spit in my face in front of 200–300 other soldiers, for example. Of course it's right to punish someone who's behaved badly, but I was punished too much, for nothing. My knees and elbows were always bleeding due to the continuous punishment. A lot of other young men were brutalized during this period of their lives too.

So, in my report, I quoted from President Hafez Al-Assad, father of the current president, when he had said: 'I don't want any of you to keep silent about any mistake or to cover up any faults.' I wrote telling them that, as a child, I had looked forward to reaching my military service, because I believed it was a service to my country and honourable. I told them I'd wanted to protect my homeland, as we'd been taught. Under Hafez Al-Assad, every morning at school, we had all had to chant a particular song, which ended with the rhyme in Arabic: 'Qa'iduna ila Al-Abad, Al-Amin Hafez Al-Assad' (it means: 'Our Leader for Ever, The Faithful Hafez Al-Assad'). It was the cult of the leader, to make us obedient, and it began in childhood.

In my report I wrote that my country could rely on me if something happened. Even though I was only a trainee, I was ready to serve my country and protect it, but instead I was humiliated over and over for no reason. When I first went into the army, I'd had high ideals, but they quickly died. This, I was sure, was the real reason behind my failure there. I was even sent to Tadmur Prison in Palmyra for forty-five days at one point. It's the most feared prison in the country, where the inmates were tortured in many brutal and degrading ways. I hate to think back on my time in the military, because it was so terrible. But what was clear was that we weren't serving our country; in reality we were pandering to the commanders, who only wanted to humiliate people. Once I was out of it, I heard this same story from lots of other men. It's well known in Syria.

*

After my military service was over, I returned to Lebanon several times for work. Lebanon, in fact, is the only foreign country I ever visited before the war. I got work at the

American University of Beirut as an electrician. Initially, I worked with a Syrian electrician in Lebanon, then I went on to work for a Lebanese man in a town in the Beqaa Valley. I'd met him in Beirut and he asked me to work with him, packaging machinery for cheese making and also fixing these machines.

At the same time, I developed my own business installing satellite dishes and also working in computer programming and formatting. I was constantly doing what I could to develop my skills and find new opportunities. Before long I had a shop as my base for installing satellite dishes, which were new in Syria at that time, in the early 1990s, soon after the Lebanese civil war, so I had a lot of business. Sometimes I also worked as a painter for short periods, and in various other jobs, basically wherever I got the chance to make some money. For example, I worked with a painter whose assistant had left him, so I was able to learn from him how to paint houses. I was a fast learner and quickly developed my knowledge in each area, gaining a little bit of experience in lots of careers. This meant I could always get work at any time. I had never stopped working since childhood, and from all this I managed to earn a very good income. I wanted to earn money, not for myself, but to help others and to have fun with my friends. I also gave money to my parents and helped pay their costs and expenses, and I paid for outings with my friends and their little brothers and sisters, taking them to fairs and playgrounds. I'm proud of how hard I worked in my youth and what I did with the money I earned.

In addition, I was later able to save money and to buy a house in eastern Aleppo, in the Al-Sha'ar neighbourhood. Once I had a house, I could get married. This is how things happen in Syria: the husband has to have a house for his wife to move into after they're married. I got married when I was twenty-five, which is relatively young in Syria. Many people don't have enough money to get married until they're forty or even older, and then they marry girls who are often a lot younger than them. As is normal in Syria, my mother chose my wife. She suggested a girl she knew very well, so I went with her to meet the girl in her parents' house in the customary way. I liked her, and we got married three months later. We went on to have three children.

★

Once I was married and settled, I applied for a job as the driver of a fire engine or an ambulance in the public sector like my father, working for the state-owned company Sadcop, but I never got the job. Two years later, in 1997, the government opened employment centres everywhere in Syria, which were meant to provide jobs in the public sector. Lots of young people applied for these jobs in these centres, and I applied again to be a fireman. I waited thirteen years, but I never got the job, even though I had the right, in theory, to get the same job as my father. Others applied for the same job after me and got it straight away, because they had *waasta*. When I asked them at the centre why I didn't get the job, they said I needed to get training as a fireman, so I put myself on a course that I paid for myself and I got an Intermediate Certificate in Rescue and Fire Fighting. But even after that, they still didn't give me the job. Someone else with connections, *waasta*, got it instead. This has always been the system.

It's ironic that it took this war in Syria for me to get the opportunity to do the work I always wanted to do, rescuing people. I've always felt it's my duty and my pleasure to help people and animals whenever they need help. I believe that whoever does this will be the happiest person in the world, besides being lucky in his life. I have believed strongly in this since childhood, that whenever I spend one lira to help people and animals, it will return to me in thousands and bring me luck. It's the most perfect work ever. Nothing compares to that happiness. I'm sure I've survived some bad accidents thanks to the blessings I've earned from my work, and I always feel strong, all because of what I'm doing for animals and for people. I'm still like Mercury/Al-Zeibaq, the cat, rushing to get food, but now I'm giving it to others instead. Fate has given me a new mission, and my life has changed completely since the start of the Syrian war.

3: How the War Began

I need to explain a little bit about the war in Syria. It's a complicated situation and many people outside the country, maybe even some inside the country, have forgotten how it all started. It was originally part of the Arab Spring, which first began, very suddenly and surprisingly, in Tunisia, right at the end of 2010 and then continued into early 2011. Most Arab countries, as you may already know, are ruled by dictators who call themselves presidents. They and their families are corrupt and they have been lining their pockets at the expense of the people for years and years. It had always seemed impossible to get rid of them, however, because their armies, police and security forces were so strong and powerful.

So, we were all amazed to watch on our TV screens as the Tunisian dictator, Ben Ali, fell from power in January 2011. There were demonstrations against him for a month, during which about a hundred people were killed, and then he just got on a plane with his wife, children, two nannies and a butler and flew to Jeddah in Saudi Arabia, where he has been, protected by the Saudi government, ever since. He had been in power for more than twenty years, but he just up and flew away. Just like that. Gone. He was accused, while absent, by the new Tunisian government of corruption, drugs trafficking and money laundering and sentenced to life imprisonment, should he ever return.

Next it was the turn of the Egyptian president, Husni Mubarak, who was ousted just weeks later in February 2011. With him, the demonstrations only lasted two weeks before he resigned, but nearly a thousand people were killed, mainly through police brutality. Mubarak had been in power for thirty years, and like our former president Hafez Al-Assad, he had been an officer in the air force, but, unlike Ben Ali, he did not run away. He was arrested and put on trial, along with his sons, and sentenced to life imprisonment for corruption. Later, in prison, he became ill and he has now been released, aged ninety.

Then it was Qaddafi's turn in Libya. He had been in power for forty-two years. The Libyan situation became rather chaotic, because Qaddafi refused to flee the country or resign like Ben Ali or Mubarak. He tried to fight back when the protests first began in February 2011, and it became very violent. But then, in April, we watched NATO go into Libya and create a no-fly zone to protect the civilians there. It was a big thing, to see the West going in to help the rebels, but, despite their efforts, about 15,000 people were killed, including Colonel Qaddafi himself, caught hiding in a sewer. In Libya to this day there is still a low-level civil war, with two governments ruling different halves of the country and lots of tribal warlords running riot, all fighting for control of the oilfields.

In Syria, watching all this happening in neighbouring countries, we were very frightened, because we knew what might happen if the Arab Spring spread to us. We had already seen what the Assad regime was prepared to do to hold onto power, as there had previously been uprisings against the ruling Ba'athist regime of the Assads, during the period when Hafez Al-Assad, father of Bashar Al-Assad, the current president, had been in charge. What happened in Hama was the bloodiest. Tens of thousands were killed on his orders in 1982, and the city centre looked like a war zone. Al-Assad senior had taken over in a military coup in 1970 and been president and head of the Armed Forces from that point until his death in June 2000. He was a clever but very ruthless man. His son Bashar became president after him and has now ruled Syria for nineteen years.

*

Since the late 1970s, Aleppo had been a major centre of opposition to the regime. In June 1979, there had even been a massacre at the Aleppo Artillery School, near where my father's company, Sadcop, was based. Over fifty unarmed Alawi cadets were shot dead by members of the Muslim Brotherhood, a conservative Sunni Muslim group banned in 1963 by the ruling Ba'athists. They called themselves the Fighting Vanguard, or *Al-Tali'a Al-Muqatila* in Arabic, and this was the first ever attack by the opposition on the ruling Alawites, the sect that Hafez Al-Assad belonged to and which most of the officers in his army belonged to as well.

So Aleppo became the target of Assad's revenge. There were running battles and clashes, with Islamist opposition groups attacking police patrols and government targets. President Assad launched a massive crackdown and there were hundreds killed. Opposition centres were raided and the government sent in its Defence Brigades, 5,000 soldiers in total, to try to keep control of the city, but even with all those troops, whole areas rebelled.

I was only four years old at the time, but I still have one abiding memory from that period. There was a curfew and no one was meant to go outside, but I was on the ground floor, sitting on the big windowsill of our house in the Old City, watching the soldiers on the street, so I jumped out of the window to go and play with them. I thought it was some game, but they shouted at me to go back home. Later I heard the sound of fighting and clashes nearby, but I didn't really understand what the sound was until my parents explained it to me.

It all got even worse after the Shaikh, the prayer leader, at the Aleppo Great Mosque was arrested. There were daily demonstrations, strikes and boycotts, with attacks on government offices. The Muslim Brotherhood were the biggest threat to the state at that time, because they were the best organized and the most heavily armed, but my parents told me there was also non-religious opposition to the Assad regime among the middle classes. In March 1980, the Muslim Brotherhood, a lot of whom were from the traditional merchant families, closed down the souks and the business district of Aleppo for two weeks. Then the strikes spread to other traditionally conservative cities, such as Hama, Homs, Idlib, Deir Ez-Zour and Al-Hasakeh.

That was when the first siege of Aleppo began, on 1 April 1980. Special Forces were sent from Damascus and from Lebanon, where we had lots of troops at that time because of the Lebanese Civil War. Over 30,000 men from various elite fighting units arrived in Aleppo to surround and seal off the city. They had hundreds of tanks and armoured vehicles that fired randomly at homes in residential areas. They sealed off whole neighbourhoods, searching house to house for weapons and suspects. The general in charge, Shafiq Fayadh, stood on his tank and shouted that he was willing to kill a thousand people a day to get rid of the Muslim Brotherhood vermin.

Detention centres were set up all over the city and a prison camp was set up in the citadel. Over the summer there were a series of massacres committed by the regime: men were rounded up haphazardly, aged fifteen and above, and shot, over 200 of them in the Souk Al-Ahad quarter alone. On the morning of Eid Al-Fitr, the religious holiday that follows the month of fasting for Ramadan, random people were ordered out of their homes in the Masharqah neighbourhood, just west of the citadel, and marched to a nearby cemetery. About a hundred were killed, mainly children, shot on the orders of the commanding officer, and several hundred more were injured. Bulldozers buried the bodies while some of them were still alive. The process was so chaotic that the dead even included some government supporters. The next day another division of troops occupied Aleppo and shot dead thirty-five more people after they had been taken from their homes in Bustan Al-Qasr, in the south-west of the city. In all about 2,000 people were killed by the security forces of the regime during the siege, and at least 8,000 were arrested and taken prisoner. The Muslim Brotherhood, for their part, killed about 300 people in Aleppo, nearly all of them Alawite officials.

Then, in June 1980, there was an assassination attempt against Hafez Al-Assad. It was organized by the Muslim Brotherhood; they threw two grenades at him while he was waiting in his guest palace in Damascus to meet an African diplomat, and fired a machine gun at him. Hafez kicked one of the grenades away, while a bodyguard threw himself on the other one and was blown to smithereens. After that, Hafez got crazy. He took huge revenge on the Muslim Brotherhood. The very next day he had a thousand prisoners in Tadmur Prison in Palmyra executed. Ten days later he passed a new law, Number 49, which meant that anyone belonging to the Muslim Brotherhood would be sentenced to death.

That siege of Aleppo lasted from April 1980 until February 1981, nearly a whole year. I was only five years old at the time, but I still have memories from those days and I still remember the fear of all the grown-ups around me. So, with all this history fresh in the memory of people like me and my parents, it's no wonder we were frightened when the Arab Spring domino effect reached Syria in 2011. It began in the south, in Deraa, near the Jordanian border, then spread to Damascus, Homs and Hama. We were all terrified about what might happen if the revolution, as we called it then, came to Aleppo.

★

At that time, I was working as an electrician. I also had a shop for electrical stuff in Hanano, which I'd had for ten years. In addition to my electrical work in people's homes and on industrial sites, I also worked at installing satellite dishes. I'd posted adverts for my shop everywhere, so it was well known all over Aleppo and my work was considered of a high standard, because I'd learnt from such a young age and was so experienced. I was really proud of my electrical shop and my work.

For a year and a half, despite the growing unrest sparked

by the Arab Spring, life went on almost as normal. In fact, Aleppo was generally considered the safest place to be, and people would come here to escape from the regime bombardments in Homs and in the suburbs of Damascus. Aleppo was the industrial and commercial capital of Syria. It was the headquarters of the national rail network, and even had its own airport ten kilometres to the east of the city centre, where there used to be international flights direct to most of the capital cities of Europe, such as Paris, London, Berlin, Athens, Stockholm and Vienna, with airlines like Lufthansa, KLM and Air France. Before the war, Aleppo had been one of the fastest-growing cities in the Middle East, with lots of people coming into the city from the outlying villages, looking for employment and better job opportunities. They came especially to areas like Shaikh Najjar, to the north of the centre beyond the ring road, where industrial zones had sprung up, catering to companies that specialized in pharmaceuticals, food processing, electrical goods manufacturing and more.

So Aleppo stayed out of the revolution at first. The memories of what had happened before were definitely a factor. We kept our heads down and tried not to get involved. The elite merchant families, most of whom are Sunni, knew it would be bad for business, so they tried to keep neutral. The Christians and other minorities also thought they would be safer sticking with the regime. They felt the regime, which claims to be secular, would look after their interests better than the uncertain future that might lie ahead with the rebels.

So perhaps it was not surprising, because of all that history, that it was at Aleppo University that the first trouble began, as the students were too young to remember the 1980 Aleppo siege or the 1982 Hama massacre. They thought the time was right, and they were full of enthusiasm for a revolution, caught up in the fever of the Arab Spring. They thought they could make the Assad regime tumble, just like the Tunisian and Egyptian and Libyan ones had before it. But the regime was ready for them and must have got wind of some of the activists there, because, in May 2012, security forces went into the university and raided the dormitories of some of the students who were suspected of being anti-regime. They confiscated the students' computers and laptops. It was all very violent and they left four students dead. The university was closed down for over a week afterwards.

The government was confident this was the way to crush all opposition, just like they had done in the 1980 siege and in Hama, but this time their fierce clampdown had the opposite effect. A few days after the university reopened, hundreds of students came out onto the university campus and held a huge anti-government protest. They thought they were safe this time, because the UN monitors had been sent into the country now. Some of them were in Aleppo, and they were even on the university campus, as part of the Peace Plan that Kofi Annan, who had been head of the UN and was now the UN's Syria Special Envoy, was trying to put in place. Three hundred of these UN monitors were meant to arrive in Syria before the end of May, then gradually hundreds more until there were a thousand of them. Their presence was meant to defuse the tensions and violence that were building all over the country, before it was too late. But it turned out it was already too late. The UN monitors had no power to stop anything. The students protesting didn't understand this, and imagined the UN monitors could protect them. They showed them the names and photos of their fellow students who had gone missing, or had been detained or maybe even been killed. They live-streamed the demonstrations on their phones, and one of the students was even recorded saying to the UN monitors: 'This is the first time we taste freedom in this country, please understand.'

The students believed that the UN would take their cause up with the government, but, instead, all that happened was that pro-government students and security forces turned on the protesters. They kicked them and beat them, and fired tear gas into the crowds of demonstrators right under the noses of the UN observers, who left and went back to their five-star hotels. They had no power to do anything else. Bashar Al-Assad, the current president and son of the president who had quashed the last uprising, even went on Russian TV to say that all the protestors were terrorists and that none of it was anything to do with an anti-government uprising. By May 2012, a year after it had all first begun, more than ten thousand civilians had been killed across the country.

It was the same wherever the UN monitors went. Local people felt braver, thinking the UN would protect them, but instead, the regime security forces just shot at them, and even attacked the UN convoys, blaming the rebels. It was a mess, and the opposition abroad was also a mess, full of disagreements, with no clear plan for what to do. The leaders of what called itself the government in exile, the Syrian National Council, kept resigning, and there were lots of rivalries and squabbles. No one knew where it was all heading, but we were really frightened, as we knew the reprisals would be violent, because it was already clear that the regime was not going to give in and resign, as had happened in Tunisia and Egypt, and also that the opposition was badly organized and not speaking with one voice.

The first serious fighting in Aleppo began between the regime Syrian army and the Free Syrian Army on 19 July 2012. The Free Army is what the soldiers called themselves after they defected from the regime army. A lot of them said they defected after they couldn't bring themselves to shoot unarmed Syrians who were demonstrating – it was a situation they'd never imagined being put in. There were also students from Aleppo University among the Free Army recruits, who had no fighting experience and so were very badly prepared. The rebels started putting up checkpoints in some of the streets, made from whatever they could find, from bags of cement to metal sheets and much more. All day for several days, there was shooting and firing between the two sides, and the internet was cut.

Then it all went quiet for a few days. The Free Army soldiers disappeared. We thought everything was getting back to normal. The shops started to reopen and people could go out again to buy food. Everyone had been too frightened to go out before. The most anyone did was to go to their neighbour's place, to talk with them, exchange information and try to understand what was going on.

Then, suddenly, the rebel fighters were back, but this time it felt different. They were more experienced, and seemed better prepared and well armed. We heard these ones were called Liwa Al-Tawheed. Most of them had long beards, and it turned out they were battalion leaders from villages and towns north and east of Aleppo, towns like Al-Bab, Manbij, Marea, Azaz and Tel Rif'at. They'd decided to unite, bypassing the leaders of the Free Syrian Army, who were now in Turkey: 'We had a meeting of all the groups in the countryside and Aleppo and we all decided we could be more powerful together. As the Liwa al-Tawheed, we decided on this mission by ourselves. The leaders in Turkey don't plan what we do, we are working on our own missions.' They had no outside help and it was all just done on the spur of the moment, with no real planning. No one was sure how many there were. Some said it was 3,000; some said it was more like 6–7,000.

All at once we lost our electricity, just as had happened in Homs. One day it was there, as normal, the next day it was gone completely. There was no time to adjust, to make preparations. It was the same with the water. Yes, there used to be water cuts anyway, especially in the summer, but usually they were only for a few hours, and we learned how to fill our tanks on the roof to prepare for the cuts. The same thing also happened with the gas cylinders we all used for cooking in our homes. Suddenly there was a shortage and everyone was scrambling to find replacements. Next the fuel disappeared, the petrol and diesel we needed for our cars. And then the *mazout* disappeared from the market, the heating fuel we needed for our houses in winter. Of course it was summer time then, so no one needed much *mazout*, but we could still see the implications unless things were resolved. Without warning, our lives were turned upside down, and most of us didn't even know who these rebels were. They'd just come in from the countryside, and we didn't really feel they were people we trusted.

We wondered, too, if taking away all our services so suddenly was maybe part of the government's plan, to make us hate the rebels. Maybe they wanted us to know immediately everything we were going to lose if we supported them? It was around this time that I started to notice more stray cats on the streets. They'd been abandoned because lots of people had started to leave their homes, trying to find safer places to go, in areas where there was no fighting, and yet, every time they moved, the fighting just caught up with them again. Most people didn't want to take sides. The rebels knew this, and told us they would only stay in the city as long as it took to get rid of the Assads and their regime. After that, they told us, they'd leave and let us build whatever kind of city we wanted.

Many of us felt some support and sympathy for the rebels. They were Sunni Muslims like us and most of them were poor. But the rich businessmen and the middle classes didn't support them, on the whole. They worried the rebels were bad for business. But we also heard stories about a few businessmen who were angry with the regime and were thinking of switching to support the rebels. The regime had made the businessmen pay money to support the military, and if they didn't pay, we heard that militias were sent to burn their storehouses. It was the sort of thing we expected from the regime, their usual threatening tactics, even down to the graffiti that appeared, which spelled it out: *Al-Assad aw ha-nahraq al-balad*/Support Assad or we'll burn the country.

★

Ordinary Syrians, the ones with no *waasta*, have suffered so much over the years from the corruption of the regime that it was inevitable that there'd be some kind of backlash, some revenge attacks on Assad's men, once the fighting started. Assad's thug militias, who were known as *shabiha*, which means 'ghosts', because they came and went in black Mercedes in their black leather jackets, all had *waasta* and exploited their privileges to the full. A lot of them were Alawites, the same religious minority as the Assads. Most of the population of Syria is Sunni Muslim – at least 70 per cent – and the Alawites, who fall broadly under the Shi'a branch of Islam, like the Iranians who support Assad, are only about 15 per cent, though no one knows the exact numbers anymore. Since the beginning of the uprising, the *shabiha* had been much more active than usual, with no limits on their cruelty or brutality. Even if there was no reason to suspect someone's disloyalty, they would still just randomly decide to victimize whole families, to make an example of them in order to warn others not even to think of disloyalty to the president, Bashar Al-Assad.

Not all *shabiha* are Alawis, the president's clan, though. In Aleppo, quite a lot of them are powerful Sunni families. In the beginning, they made their money from sheep trading, then some of them became smugglers, first of pharmaceuticals, then of narcotics. A few were jailed before the war, when their activities were too much even for the state, but in practice, they were part of the state, like a shadowy arm. Even from inside prison, they were still drugs lords, keeping up their lucrative illegal businesses.

Assad, therefore, did a deal when the fighting first

started. He offered them amnesty, giving them weapons and salaries, if they would be his mafia in the city. So they did. They threatened rich businessmen, forcing them to give money to the state, they took hostages, attacked students at Aleppo University, and carried out robberies and assassinations.

As their power grew, the Free Syrian Army decided to retaliate, killing out of revenge. I could understand why. We all could. But we knew it wouldn't solve anything. We knew it would probably only make things worse, like stirring up a hornets' nest. And we were the ones who suffered, the innocent civilians who had never chosen any of this.

And of course things did get worse. The western media started calling it 'Syria's Stalingrad'. I didn't know exactly what had happened in Stalingrad or why, but I knew that the city ended up destroyed. We all feared this is what would happen to Aleppo too. Later, I learned that the Stalingrad battle had only lasted about five months. Our battle was to last nearly four and a half years, and became the bloodiest of the whole of the Syrian war. I learned that soldiers going into Stalingrad used to say: 'We are entering hell.' After two or three days there they said: 'No, this isn't hell. This is ten times worse than hell.'

That is what my hometown, Aleppo, became. Worse than hell.

4: Alaa Ambulance

I consider myself to be neutral in this war. I'm not with one side or another, except for the side of poor people, the innocent victims in all this, who aren't guilty or responsible in any way for what happened. So, when the conflict first reached Aleppo, I wanted to help these people. I had my own minivan, which I realized I could use as an ambulance. From the summer of 2012 onwards, for a year and a half, I worked alone, doing rescue work in Aleppo. I was completely independent; I used my own money, including savings, to pay for fuel and repairs to my car. People used to call me Alaa Ambulance.

Early on there'd been lots of clashes and fighting in the area of Al-Sha'ar, where I'd bought my first house. I'd been living there for three years when the revolution began, but now, like so many other people, we had to leave. I took my wife and children to a relation's house in Hanano, and we stayed there for about a week to ten days. Then I rented a house close by for about four months, and after that we moved to another house in the same area. I'm calling it a house, but it was actually just a flat in a faceless concrete block, that cheap Soviet-era style of housing from the 1970s and 1980s, under Hafez Al-Assad, of which we had so much in Syria. The owners had left, so I paid them for the first three months, but after that they didn't take any more rent from me, because they'd left the country and weren't returning, so I was able to live there rent-free.

The area where we were living in north-east Aleppo was known as Masaken Hanano, which means Hanano Housing. It's a very big area, one of the biggest areas of informal housing in Syria, and the neighbourhood where we lived was called Al-Haidarieh. After the war, it was the first area to be zoned off for development, in October 2018. It had been flattened by regime and Russian bombs and emptied of residents. Our block had five floors and we lived on the second floor. People didn't like to live on the upper floors of a building at this time, as the top floor was always more exposed to shelling. The ground floor was also bad, because whenever a shell fell, the whole of the ground floor area was affected, so everyone preferred to live on the middle floors. Some people, if their block of flats had a basement, would even choose to live there, to be safer from the bombing.

I still remember clearly the very first person I ever rescued in my minivan. It was right at the beginning of the crisis in Aleppo, when the regime army was withdrawing from the Haidarieh neighbourhood in Hanano, where we were living, and the opposition fighters were taking over.

There was random shelling and the fighting had just started. Everyone stayed indoors where it was safe, but I went out to see if anyone in the street was injured. I saw people running towards the park not far from my house. There was an injured person there. So I ran there too, but there's a highway, the main thoroughfare of Hanano, that I had to cross in order to reach the park. It was difficult to do so, because it's the road that the regime army uses to move around the area, and there were regime tanks on the highway about 2,000 metres away, but I managed to cross it, despite the shelling, and reached the park to help the injured person, a civilian. All the houses around there were full of civilians and some other people had come out to try to help him too – maybe they were his relatives? But there was no car to transfer him, and he had a bullet in his thigh. His flesh was all torn and his intestines were hanging out, so I told them to put him on my back and I carried him back across the highway. They didn't follow, because they were afraid of the regime's tanks, but I ran with the injured person on my back for about 600 or 700 metres, until I reached my car. I laid him on the back seat and drove through the underpasses until I left the area. I drove to Helwanieh, on the road to Al-Bab, and took him to the Dar Al-Shifaa Hospital. That was the first time I ever rescued someone.

I wished that I could have done this work without a war taking place, but it made me very happy to have helped that man. My ambition to help with rescue and ambulance work had come true. After thirteen years of waiting for this job, having had my application rejected again and again, I was finally able to do it independently of the government. Of course I wasn't the only one. There were many others like me. Sometimes we made jokes if there was no shelling, saying things like: 'There's no work today!' We considered it as work but we were all passionate about it.

On top of my rescue work, I also kept working as an electrician for the first four months of the crisis in Aleppo. My shop was open, but there wasn't much work. No one was thinking about electrical installations, so I used to leave my brother-in-law to look after the place, while I would drive off in my car, using it like an ambulance for rescuing people who needed help. In the early days, there weren't always many casualties, and the bombings were infrequent, but there was often fighting and there were lots of skirmishes in the surrounding neighbourhoods. During these early stages, before the horrific jet bombing that came later, we used to move around freely, and all the shops were open.

So my work as an ambulance driver and a rescue man began right from the start of the crisis in Aleppo, but my love for cats also continued. It never stopped. I always helped any stray cats in the street, especially the ones that were ill. I used to treat them by giving them children's medicine, maybe not the best method but we didn't have anything better. I would dissolve an antibiotic pill of 250 milligrammes in water and give it to them, for example, a technique I'd learned from my father. I treated pet house cats sometimes as well, not just strays. In the area of Zibdiyeh, I found a pet cat that had difficulty breathing. With the owner's permission, I used to go to the house where it lived and put serum in its nose to help it to breathe. We didn't know how else to treat it, so I just did the best I could for him. All this experience helping sick cats gradually built up over time until I managed to become almost like a paramedic. I learnt on the job and helped a lot of animals.

*

In Islam, there are six commandments telling Muslims to care for animals, to feed them and look after them. These *hadith*, or commandments, also tell us about how the Prophet behaved during his lifetime and what he told his companions, people similar to those whom Christians call 'disciples'. From all this we know that the Prophet Muhammad liked animals, and especially cats, very much. One *hadith* says the Prophet Muhammad cut the sleeve off his coat when he needed to get up to pray, rather than disturb the cat that was sleeping on it. Another *hadith* says that when a cat gave birth on his coat, he then looked after the kittens.

A lot of these *hadith* sayings come from one of his companions, whose real name was Abd al-Rahman, but who was always known as Abu Huraira, the Kitten Man or 'Father of the Kitten', because, like Muhammad, he liked cats very much and often carried a kitten round inside his coat to play with and keep him company. He'd arrived in Medina poor and destitute along with others from his tribe, but the Prophet Muhammad liked him because of his love of animals and put him in charge of the camels. There's even a story that Abu Huraira once saved Muhammad's life. When Muhammad was about to be bitten by a poisonous snake, Abu Huraira quickly brought out the cat from inside his coat, so that the cat could kill the snake just in time. Muhammad touched the head of the cat in thanks afterwards, and folklore says this is why many cats have four stripes on their heads; they're the marks of the Prophet's fingers.

In the Quran it says God created animals to give us warmth and food and other benefits, to carry our burdens. It says we must look after them, feed them and bring them home to rest after their work. When we treat animals well and help them, we get a great reward from God. It even tells us in the Quran that all the animals and birds on earth will be resurrected and gathered before God at the final judgement, and that they're all just communities like our own.

I've had lots of arguments with people about this, people who get angry with me for defending animals. Honestly, I don't like these kinds of arguments and prefer not to get involved, but at the same time I can't be neutral when I see someone treating animals badly. Once I saw a man tie a dog to a motorbike and drag it along. Another time I saw a cat with a metal chain tied to its tail. The cat couldn't move. In both cases, I couldn't be silent. They were hurting these animals so badly with their cruel behaviour. I'm one of very few people in this part of the world who helps animals, but I don't do it just because it's in accordance with the commandments of the Prophet and Islam, but also because I'm a human being. If I can help an animal, why not, as long as this animal doesn't hurt me? Whenever I help an animal, God will reward me.

*

Once the crisis began, a lot of cats needed care and compassion. Their owners left and they were abandoned. A month after the war had begun in Aleppo, I noticed a white cat in the street. I recognized it and knew it belonged to a Kurdish man who'd left Aleppo on the first day of the crisis to seek safety in Afrin, a Kurdish area in Syria, north of Aleppo and close to the Turkish border. He'd left with his family as soon as the first fighters had entered the part of Hanano where we lived, and clearly he'd just abandoned his cat in the street.

The poor cat looked very dirty and I felt sorry for her. I opened a tin of sardines and gave it to her, then I took her home with me. She was the first cat I took home with me after the war began. I called her Lulu, in honour of my white cat from childhood.

*

When Eid al-Fitr began at the end of Ramadan, in August 2012, instead of the usual celebrations, the shops stayed shuttered up and no one ventured out for the usual Eid visits to relatives, friends and neighbours. The rebels had been in the city for about a month, around 3,000 of them, fighting for control of the south-west, in the Saif Al-Dawla District. Air strikes from Syrian fighter jets and helicopters had by then displaced the rebels from their stronghold in the Salaheddin District. Regime forces pushed in with tanks, then there was fighting street to street, room to room. More and more people whose homes were on the frontline evacuated, taking what possessions they could and leaving. The state newspaper *Al-Watan*, which means 'the Motherland', reported that 'the Mother of all Battles' had started. They were right.

I had been carrying on with bits and pieces of electrical work, installing rechargeable lights and solar panels in people's homes for free, especially for people in my neighbourhood, but I didn't go to my shop much. I just used to go there at night to collect any money my brother-in-law and my other employee had taken in and to give them their wages. Then we'd close the shop and go home. As the situation in Aleppo got worse, and more and more people began to get displaced, fewer and fewer customers came to the shop. In the end we closed it, five months after the start of the crisis. By then I wasn't getting much by way of income from it anyway, but I had my savings, which amounted to 1,200,000 Syrian pounds, about US$24,000. I'd been saving this amount to buy another vehicle. My ambulance work continued, but it was voluntary and therefore unpaid, so I started to spend my own savings on the necessities of life, things that were becoming scarce.

Most of the people in my area had already left, but about 2,000 people, including women and children, stayed behind in the neighbourhood. When we cooked our food, we didn't use gas or diesel, as it was too precious. We cooked on firewood instead to save diesel and gas. It caused a lot of soot and smoke, but we were trying as much as possible to save fuel. We needed diesel not just for our vehicles but also for our generators. We had three generators that I'd bought for US$7,500. We used them to generate electricity for the houses in our neighbourhood and I rigged up an electricity network. The network was connected to my house and there was an electrical circuit for each house in the neighbourhood. I gave each house a capacity of one ampere. The capacity of the bigger generator was eighty amperes, but we hardly used it, because it needed too much diesel – about 0.5 to 0.75 litres to run it for just an hour. I had a smaller one which consumed less and which we used in the underground areas where we took shelter during the bombing. I also had a Lister Petter generator that I used to pump water out of the wells. In summer, I would turn on the electricity from 5 a.m. until 10 a.m., but not in the winter until it got dark at 4.30 p.m., as that's when we used most of our water.

Everyone at that time had to make a difficult decision about whether to stay or go. Nobody really wanted to leave their city, but some people moved to nearby areas where there were no clashes, hoping that, if they just moved further away, they'd be safe. My family decided to stay in the neighbourhood. I wanted to be close to people, in order to help them in whatever way I could. Often people got caught up in places where clashes broke out, either because they lived there or because they just happened to be visiting or shopping in those areas when the bombardments started.

I often helped people who wanted to move from one place to another, but who had no transport, as they were poor. But there weren't many vehicles moving around on the streets anyway. Most of the taxis had stopped working, because any moving vehicle could become a target for both sides, the opposition *and* the regime. I helped a lot of people this way, while at the same time always carrying on with my hobby of feeding any cats I found, and helping them.

By late 2012 and early 2013, the fighting had reached the Great Mosque and the old souks beside it. This was the old city centre, *Al-Madina* as we call it; the place where I had danced in the sunlight as a child. This was the area where most of the fighting was concentrated, along with the mixed Muslim and Christian area called Al-Jdaideh, and of course the citadel. The rebels were always trying to take the citadel, because it was the obvious natural defence and highest point around. It's on a circular volcano-like mound right in the middle of the city, with a deep moat all around it. There hasn't been any water in the moat for a long time, not for centuries, but it's still a deep gully that anyone would have to cross to get inside. This moat, and the steep ramp leading up to the strong walls and the main gateway, was all built by Saladin's son, Al-Malik Az-Zahir Ghazi, as a base against the Crusaders in the Middle Ages. The main gateway at the top of the entrance ramp is very strong, with five separate inner iron gates to protect the people inside.

As a child, I used to love to go up into the citadel, especially in summer, and catch the cooling breezes while enjoying the views over the city. The souks were unmistakeable, spread out at the foot of the citadel, with their distinctive stone domes and roofs. I remember the first gates had serpent dragons carved on them to frighten the enemy, and the inner gates had smiling lions and sad lions that were meant to have magical powers and to protect against evil. Inside there were lots of dungeons too, dark frightening places where lots of prisoners had ended their days. Some of them had been built as water cisterns originally. One of the big ones was called the Prison of Blood and at school we were told some famous Crusaders had died there. The French used it as a prison too, when they controlled Syria for twenty-six years under the French Mandate after the First World War.

So, whoever was in power always controlled the city from the citadel, and therefore the regime always held the citadel. Before the war, it had been like an open-air museum with a nice cafe inside, but they turned it back into an army barracks and military base, just like it had been designed for centuries ago. They probably used the prisons too.

In the years before the war, when Syria and Aleppo were starting to develop tourism, the Agha Khan Development Network restored and renovated a lot of Aleppo's historic monuments, the citadel among them – I learned at school that the city had over 800 officially recognized historic monuments, which, I feel, shows how rich Aleppo must have been in times gone by. The Agha Khan NGO is an independent cultural charity and it invested a lot of money in Old Aleppo, trying to improve the neighbourhood and give people some green space to enjoy – they made a big pedestrianized area, for example, to make the city centre nicer for people to sit in, away from the traffic and fumes. There were also lots of other efforts to preserve the ancient centre and save it from developers and town planners, all of whom wanted to knock old buildings down to make new roads, and in 1986, when I was eleven, Aleppo became a UNESCO World Heritage Site.

The pedestrianized area was the first time Aleppo had ever had somewhere where cars were not allowed. At first we weren't sure about the idea. We were used to being able to drive everywhere. But gradually we really liked it. A whole cluster of cafes and simple restaurants grew up just by the foot of the ramp up into the citadel in the 2000s. They became very popular places for young people to meet. It was a new thing, with young women going there to smoke the *arghileh* (*shisha*). It was the first time people had seen women smoking in public places. After that, it became a habit for everyone.

These cafes, as well as being opposite the citadel, were also right by the entrance to the old souks, in the heart of Aleppo's Old City. Our old souks were famous around the world and the biggest in the region, crammed with thousands of shops. Only donkeys, mopeds and bicycles could fit in these alleyways alongside the shoppers. All our famous Aleppo handicrafts were on sale there, things like silks and other textiles, all decorated with beautiful embroidery. There were also the famous soaps, made from natural laurel and olive oil, in all shapes and sizes, as well as wooden boxes inlaid with mother of pearl.

But the souk was not just aimed at the tourists. We Aleppans used to shop there too, for meat and fruit and vegetables, as well as all other kinds of food. Syria produces all its own fruit and vegetables – the countryside around Aleppo is surrounded by fruit, nut and olive orchards. We're self-sufficient, growing everything we need in our fertile river valleys in the Orontes and the Euphrates, and these fresh natural ingredients are what we use for all our cooking. We love fresh food. Tomatoes, aubergines, courgettes and onions are the basics for us, and used in almost all our dishes, like the delicious ones my mother used to make for all the family at home, flavoured with *za'atar*.

Aleppo was very famous for its cuisine, based on this fresh produce, which we claimed was the best in all Syria. Our style of cooking is different and more exotic than other cities. I think it's because of our special mix of different people. We all learnt from each other – the Armenians, the Kurds, the Arab Christians, the Circassians and the Turcomans. We have more than twenty different kinds of *Kebab Halabi*, Aleppo Kebab, and even simple foods like falafel and beans, what we call *fool* in Arabic, are delicious. On Fridays after prayers, we'd head to the souks to eat falafel from Al-Faihaa, a special place in Baron Street, or sometimes *fool* from Abu Abdu's place in Al-Jdaideh, near Dar Zamaria. I liked my *fool* with lemon, not with the sesame paste we call *tahini*, because it was lighter. If I had it with *tahini*, I couldn't move or work afterwards. Everyone used to eat at Abu Abdu's small place. Even Bashar Al-Assad went there once. It made the best *fool* in Aleppo, but during the war it was on the frontline and heavily damaged. Abu Abdu died recently, may he rest in peace. Everyone knew him.

But my favourite food in all the world is called Kebbeh Safar Jaalieh, which is a special Aleppo dish. They have it in Idlib too, but not in Damascus or other parts of Syria. My mother used to make it on special occasions, like at religious holidays, or if we had relatives or guests visiting. It's a very rich, delicious dish made from lamb and cubes of quince, all cooked in a sour sauce, with rice at the side. We had this kind of expensive dish very rarely, but I remember it most at Eid, on the first day of holiday after a month of fasting during Ramadan. We even used to give our cats some of it, I remember, because it was full of meat.

Over 40,000 people used to work in Aleppo's famous souks. There were the butchers, with carcasses of animals hanging right in front of your nose. There were the perfume shops with shelves full of delicate glass bottles where you could try out scents with exotic names, all made from local products, such as jasmine, rose and sandalwood. The stone vaulted roofs kept the place cool even in summer, keeping out the weather and making the networks of passages into a real maze of smells and fragrances.

And that, of course, is why the rebels first came to the souks. They were the perfect maze in which to hide, the perfect place to escape detection and regime snipers. And people didn't live there, so there were no local residents to disturb. The armed rebel fighters set up their headquarters in one of the old bathhouses, right in the heart of the souks, thinking it would be safe and that they could move around without being seen from the air. But the regime army just fired shells and artillery at the souks, and one of them hit an electricity sub-station, setting it on fire. The fire spread quickly to the souks all around, and so, in just one night, all the merchandise and wooden doors went up in smoke, making tens of thousands of people bankrupt, just like that.

It wasn't deliberate. Both sides were to blame, the regime *and* the rebels. But as usual, it was the ordinary people, the shopkeepers and the shoppers, who suffered most. Early on in the fighting, I saw one of the young rebels stop an old man. He was just trying to get to the mosque for prayers, but there was fighting in the streets and they said he should go back home. He looked tired and confused, poor guy. The young rebel got him a cup of water, then asked him: 'Who is better, the regime army or the Free Syrian Army?' The old man waved his arms helplessly and said: 'I swear I don't know. You are all my sons.'

But we were all shocked when, in April 2013, the famous old minaret of the Great Mosque suddenly came crashing down. Its stones smashed into the courtyard. It was a thousand years old, from Seljuk times, the only Seljuk minaret in all of Syria, and was very beautiful, with lots of stone carving and inscriptions. Of course the regime blamed the rebels for the minaret's destruction. They said the rebels had blown it up by putting mines underneath it. Quite why the rebels would do that, I don't know. And, of course, the rebels blamed the regime in turn. They said that, before being pushed out of the Great Mosque, the regime soldiers had laid mines under the minaret. Then, from the citadel and from other buildings nearby, they had tried over and over to explode the mines by firing artillery at them, until they finally succeeded.

We don't know for sure what happened. What we do know is that the rebels, while they controlled the mosque, did try to protect it and the precious things inside it. They dismantled the historic wooden *minbar* – what Westerners call a pulpit – and took it away to a safe place to protect it from fire. There are videos of them doing this that were taken at that time. Later, when the regime retook the mosque, they accused the rebels of selling the *minbar* in Turkey.

Rebel students from Aleppo University also built a special wall from breezeblocks in front of the tomb of Zachariah inside the mosque. Zachariah is the father of John the Baptist, and in Islam we consider him a holy man too. Sometimes we even call the mosque *Al-Zakariyeh* after him. The tomb has beautiful blue and turquoise tiles that are over 500 years old and they were getting hit by regime snipers firing into the mosque from a building nearby, which is why the students built the wall, with a special bomb-blast cloth behind it. They also built a special protective wall around the medieval sundial in the courtyard. It was out in the open, exposed, and could easily have been damaged. But they put sandbags all round it, then built the wall and sealed it all up with padlocks. This protects it to this day, as it's still inside that protective wall.

I used to go to the Great Mosque regularly as a boy with

my father and have many fond memories, things like how the women tourists were given special long hooded robes to wear over their western clothes before they were allowed to enter. Aleppo has hundreds of mosques, but the Great Mosque is the special one, the biggest and most important one. Every single one of Aleppo's mosques has been damaged in this war, but only twelve have been destroyed beyond repair. The rest can be saved. The priority, of course, is the Great Mosque. The regime must repair this one first, but it doesn't have the money. So Russia persuaded the Muslim Chechen Republic, part of the Russian Federation, to fund the cost. The Chechen president is a strongman like Putin, and the Chechens are Sunnis, like most Syrians. The mosque is now being repaired as fast as possible. There's even a plan to rebuild the minaret, using the old stones and some plans made by the Italians back in the 1990s.

*

When the first barrel bombs started to be dropped in Aleppo in 2013, a small girl brought me her pet cat, Zahra. The name means 'Flower' and she's a female cat, a very pretty grey colour. We call this colour 'zaitouni' in Arabic, which means 'like an olive'. It is a very common colour for cats in Syria. The little girl came with her father because, like many people, they had decided to leave the country, as their home had been completely destroyed by the heavy bombardment. They'd heard that I took care of cats. They couldn't take the cat with them to Turkey, because they were smuggling themselves into Turkey illegally, so it was going to be impossible to smuggle the cat with them. But they didn't want to just abandon her in the street, so they were looking for a safe place for the cat to stay and they knew that I was feeding cats and helping them. They told their daughter that the best thing would be to leave the cat with me. Then, if the war ended, they would return to take her back.

The girl asked me: 'Can I take her back if I return?' I replied: 'Of course you can.' I told them it would be my pleasure to keep the cat and to look after her, but that I couldn't guarantee she wouldn't run away. The father said: 'It's totally fine. We know you're taking care of cats, so you won't leave or get rid of her. We trust you'.

The family was leaving in about five days, so the little girl came every day to see the cat. Zahra liked the little girl a lot. She used to run to her every time she came, but, after five days, they left and the cat stayed with me. The girl said goodbye so tenderly that she made everyone around her cry too, including me and the two friends with me at the time.

Zahra stayed with us for about four months. I hope that she was happy to have a home during that time, rather than being out on the streets, but it was still a dangerous place to be. One day, during shelling of the area, Zahra was hit by shrapnel and died, poor creature. The girl called me regularly from Turkey to ask me about the cat, and I always told her Zahra was fine. I didn't tell her that Zahra had been killed. I told her my phone didn't take good photos any more. This was my excuse for not sending her new photos of Zahra. I didn't want her to feel sad, so I kept telling her the cat was fine. I didn't know how to explain to her about Zahra's death.

Zahra was a very calm and nice cat, and very beautiful, because the girl had taken such good care of it. When they first brought the cat to me, I asked the girl: 'Where did you get this lovely cat from?' She explained: 'My little brother brought it for me from our uncle's house. It was a present because he knows I like cats so much. He's only seven, but he got our parents' permission first,' she laughed. The story of Zahra is very sad. It had a big impact on me.

With all the destruction and what was happening in Aleppo, you can see why Zahra's family never came back. Like most Aleppo families, they had to stay away in Turkey. Aleppo used to have three and a half million inhabitants. Now it has less than two million. The population has nearly halved, and most of those who have left are Sunni Muslims like me. And, as long as Assad is in charge, we cannot return, as we will be accused of being 'terrorists', all because we lived in East Aleppo.

Aleppo became the biggest disaster of the Syrian war. It was a terrible mistake for the rebels to enter the city. It was a rich place, always working and trading, but once it entered the war, thieves appeared, wanting to steal from all the factories and businesses. In Arabic we say that it became 'tharwa laysat thawra', which is a play on words and means that the fighting became about 'making a fortune not a revolution'. Many people made fortunes. The leaders of the militant groups now have hotels and restaurants in Turkey, leaving the poor to do the fighting on small salaries. The war brought the city to its knees.

5: The Cat Man of Aleppo

My daily routine during those first three years of the war, from 2012 onwards, was beyond anything I'd ever experienced before. Not just for me, of course, but for everyone in Aleppo. From that point on, I don't recall ever being able to sleep at a regular time. My days were completely disorganized. I could never have any routine, because I had to be ready to help at all times of the day and night.

I was the only one who had an ambulance in besieged Aleppo at the beginning. Some of us had bought handheld radios, so that we could communicate when the mobile network was down, and I'd get a call on this radio, asking me to rescue people. But even if there wasn't a call, I used to wake up early and go directly to work, by which I mean my work in ambulance and rescue. I'd wait in a place near an area I knew was being targeted; I waited there until they bombed it, then I helped rescue any casualties.

On my way back home again after these informal shifts, I used to drop off food for cats, picking up a sandwich from a street vendor for myself as well on the way. Sometimes I'd take some bread home with me, and some *labneh* (a kind of thick yogurt), plus tomatoes and cucumbers, for breakfast. I'd also do the rounds of the meat shops and the butchers, who knew me. They'd give me the leftovers for my cats, meat that a human couldn't eat and which might otherwise have gone to waste, as I was looking after about sixty stray or abandoned cats by then. Once they'd been fed, I'd go to check up on the kids in the neighbourhood, and play games with them, games like football and hide and seek.

Then, in the evenings, I'd give the cats their food again, as I tried to keep to a routine and feed them twice a day, at specific times, generally 2 p.m. and at 7 p.m. The cats would wait for me at those two fixed times to eat, because they knew that was the usual pattern. But sometimes it didn't work out like that, as people could call me on my mobile or on my radio at any time, if there was an emergency. So the cats often had to wait until whenever I got back.

Because I was always so short of sleep, I tried to find opportunities during the day to take naps, and this became my daily routine for almost five years. I washed my clothes whenever I could, but most of the time there was no electricity or water. The only water to be had was from the wells, since, at that time, ISIS – we call these Islamic extremists *Daesh* in Arabic – were occupying the water source in the Khafseh area, close to the Euphrates dam on Lake Assad. This lake is the main source of Aleppo's water supply. ISIS had cut off the supply for both sides, for the regime *and* the opposition. As a rule, most cities in Syria get their domestic water from springs, wells and ground-water, except Aleppo, which gets its water piped in from Lake Assad, the big reservoir on the Euphrates. Therefore, for my neighbourhood, and for all the residents of Aleppo, the only water we now had access to was from wells, and we had to boil the water and then wait for it to cool down so that it was clean enough to use. Sometimes, if we had them, we would use chlorine pills to clean the water, but they weren't readily available.

I continued like this for nearly three full years, rescuing people and feeding cats and going about my daily life as best I could. Then, in late 2015, people started to notice me and to talk about me. My reputation had grown somehow, and Syrians both inside and outside the country were mention-ing me and what I was doing.

It all began with a British journalist reporting from Aleppo. He asked me if he could write a report about what I was doing, and he was surprised to discover that I had about sixty or seventy cats in front of where I lived, so he wrote an article about me, describing my job in rescue and as an ambulance driver, as well as my role in animal welfare. That was the turning point. From that stage on, people abroad began to know who I was and the purpose of my work during this tragic war: to take care of animals and people, rather than run away and save myself. The main message of the journalist's report was: 'Here is a man who takes care of people, saves people and takes care of cats. He stays while others leave.'

After that many more articles started to appear about me, and television channels sent journalists to interview me about what I was doing. Through those news channels, even more people outside of Syria got to know me. People began to ask about 'the cat man of Aleppo'.

★

It was around this time that I met Ernesto, a very special cat. Our story together coincided with the start of the cat sanctuary, the first cat sanctuary not just in Syria but, I believe, in the whole Arab world.

In 2015, while I was working as an ambulance driver in Hanano on the north-eastern outskirts of Aleppo, I saw a man carrying a bag with a young ginger cat in it.

'What's the problem with this cat?' I asked him.

'We don't want him anymore,' he said. 'We want to get rid of him because we can't afford to feed him. We can hardly find food for ourselves.'

It turned out he lived in an unofficial housing area, what we call a 'random' area, because they just spring up haphazardly, as kind of slums, where poor people from the countryside have come to the city to find work and food. Even as long ago as 1970, the national census showed that 39 per cent of Aleppo's population were rural migrants to the city. The expansion of the city had been rather chaotic and unregulated, and a lot of people ended up working in the factories that were also expanding in the north-east in the new industrial zones and living in these slums.

This man was obviously very poor and had decided to take the cat to a place as far away as possible so that they didn't have to feed it anymore. 'The cat doesn't live in our house,' he explained, 'but he just comes to us anytime he feels hungry and needs to eat. The children get upset when we have to turn him away.' At that time there was heavy bombardment and fighting in their area, so everybody struggled to get food. He said he and his family were full of despair, but they couldn't afford to move to a safer place because they had no money. They used to share their food with this cat, but now they didn't even have enough to do that.

I fully understood how hard it was for this man and his family, so I asked him if I could take the cat instead and he said yes. I took the cat out of the bag, put him in the car and took him home with me. The cat was extremely hungry, so I gave him a lot of food and water. Even though cats don't often drink much water, as they get most of their hydration from the water in their food, he really needed it. I liked this ginger cat a lot, so I brought him indoors with me, rather than leaving him outside with the other cats. I felt sorry for him and for the way he'd lost the family who used to take care of him, and he seemed to like me a lot in return and always wanted me to cuddle him. He used to sleep on my shoulders, follow me around and always sit close to me.

It just so happened that this little cat's arrival in my life coincided with the start of the increased interest in me and my humanitarian work in Aleppo. After that first report by the British journalist, lots of other people tried to contact me.

Some of the people who got in contact with me asked me to share photos of my ambulance work and also of my work with animals, so I started to send them pictures of myself and of my cats, and of the people I was helping every day. It wasn't difficult and I thought nothing of it. But, thanks to these pictures and the publicity they got, the Karam Organization contacted me and offered to help me buy a new ambulance. Then people from an NGO called Syria Charity contacted me. They'd heard that my car kept getting damaged and broken, and after my car was completely destroyed, they sent me a replacement car to use. They even offered me a monthly salary, as a contribution to my costs. I didn't ask for any of this, but they told me they wanted to help me with my work. And it wasn't just me doing ambulance work by this time – there were many of us, all beginners in this work and unpaid volunteers – and this NGO paid us salaries and covered the costs of running the cars. I wasn't part of the Syrian Civil Defence – what you in the West later called the 'White Helmets', after the US and UK governments started to fund them – but we often worked alongside them. We all helped each other out wherever possible, as we shared a common aim.

*

Among the volunteers there was a sixteen-year-old boy called Ahmad, who helped me and also the Civil Defence. His father had died and he was the only boy among three girls in his family. His mother did everything she could to try to stop him going out to help, but he liked his rescue work too much. One day, a barrel bomb hit the Haydarieh Roundabout, a busy area where minibuses and street sellers gathered, and Ahmad was among the first to reach the injured, but then the helicopter came round a second time, and dropped another barrel bomb in the same place. This was a new tactic. Before this, they would generally only drop one bomb before moving on to drop others elsewhere. A lot of people had run to help the injured and were caught in the blast when the second bomb fell. Ahmad was among those killed.

I wasn't there that day, praise be to God. I'd rescued three people in my car earlier and transferred them to the hospital, so that was where I was when I heard the news that Ahmad had fallen as a martyr. I couldn't quite believe it, as he was such a familiar sight – the chubby teenager in blue overalls. We used to spoil him and give him food, and he was so courageous. He was the first person to be martyred in the Civil Defence.

So, from that day onwards, we began to be more careful and would wait for the helicopter to leave the area before rushing in to help. We worked out that it took three minutes for it to complete its circuit, so we knew we had to move people within those three minutes. If we were still there, we might be among the second round of victims and those of us who had gone to rescue people might then need other people to rescue us in turn.

*

One of the most difficult and upsetting things about our rescue work was not having time to carry injured people properly. I know the proper ways of carrying people – such as putting them on a stretcher – but we had to evacuate places too quickly. We had to run with them from the place under bombardment in order to avoid the second shelling, so there was no time to get the stretcher and, even if there had been, the stretcher needed two people to carry it. We often fell to the ground while we were carrying the injured too. I'm sure there were people who were hurt further because of the way we carried them, or the way we pulled them out from under the rubble or the way we transferred them to the hospital, but we had to try. And, thanks to the help of Syria Charity, at least I was able to do what I could to help. Their salary meant I could enlarge the ambulance system and the team of people who were helping me. I formed a whole team, about ten of us in all, as well as the volunteers, and together we collected old and broken cars and fixed them so that we could use them as ambulances. Gradually we built our fleet up to twelve ambulances, which we made into a network spread across Aleppo.

Also around this time, as I was expanding the ambulance set up, a woman called Alessandra Abidin contacted me. She too was interested in my story, so we started to speak regularly. Alessandra was living in Italy, and has Italian nationality, but she is half Lebanese, so could speak to me in Arabic. She asked me a lot about the way I was helping cats during the conflict, and she offered to create a social media profile for me, using Facebook and Twitter.

'There are people who are asking about you, so why don't we create a group through whom we can communicate with people?' she said. 'We can raise funds to help you create a cat sanctuary. I'll help you by translating everything you do, so that you can communicate with people. So many people are asking about you. They want to make sure that you're ok, they want to know about your situation, and about what's happening with you and about what's bothering you and so on. They care about you. They want to know your daily news and to hear stories about any cats you find.'

At first I told her I didn't need her help. I told her I could feed these cats out of the salary I already had. It only cost me four dollars a day, so I could feed the cats at my own expense. I'd always fed cats by spending my own money, after all, so I didn't feel I needed help from anybody. I didn't care about Facebook or Twitter, because I didn't have any leisure time. I was working day and night, helping people.

But then she explained more: 'It's not just for you. If we set up a cat sanctuary, we can help you for other people's sake, and help other people who are in need. We'll support you. Maybe other people can benefit from your experience? Don't stay unknown. If you say nothing, nobody will know anything about you.'

I thought about it and, in the end, I agreed.

So Alessandra created the Facebook group 'Il Gattaro d'Aleppo', which means 'The Cat Man of Aleppo' in Italian, and a Twitter account called @theAleppoCatman. More and more people joined the group and followed the feed, and I started to communicate with them via Alessandra (most of them were European and didn't speak Arabic).

As we were discussing the practicalities of all this and she was explaining how they could raise funds to help me with my humanitarian work, she mentioned in passing that she'd had a cat she loved very much but who had died of cancer. He had been called Ernesto. In return, I told her the story of the new ginger cat I'd just rescued from the man in the street who could no longer afford to feed it. I said that, if we were going to start a cat sanctuary in Aleppo, we should call it Ernesto's, after her cat, and that I would call this new cat Ernesto too, in tribute. That made her very happy, and that was how we came to call this new initiative 'Ernesto's Sanctuary for Cats'.

Alessandra has since become one of my best friends. She has helped and supported me so much, providing me with lots of much needed health information about cats and other animals and so much more. Feeding cats in the street had been my hobby, but it was thanks to Alessandra's suggestion that I started to do so much more. It was her idea that I should set up the sanctuary especially for cats so that I had somewhere to bring cats and protect them, not just to feed them.

This first Ernesto's sanctuary was in Hanano, where I lived at that time, in the extreme north-east of Aleppo, which was far away from the fighting at the beginning. The location I found was a wide empty space with many trees. I was able to get it up and running in a basic way within fifteen days. I managed to buy the land opposite my house and then I prepared it to become the cat sanctuary. I didn't come up against any difficulties, and I was able to get drilling and levelling machinery to prepare the ground. Before the war, there hadn't been many people living in Hanano, only about 300,000 before the war, but once the war started, the area had become more and more crowded as people moved out there to escape the fighting in the areas where they'd been living nearer the city centre, just as I'd done when I moved from my house in Al-Sha'ar. I was lucky to find the space. Almost half a million extra people moved

to live in Hanano during the war. It became a heavily populated quarter.

★

As Alessandra had predicted, the cat sanctuary helped to
make people outside of Syria more aware of the difficulties
we were facing in Aleppo. It wasn't just cats we were helping; thanks to the donations from the people all over the
world, from as far away as South Korea and Japan, we were
also able to support more than 2,000 people in our neighbourhood. Roughly every fifteen days we used to distribute
food to 120 families. We gave them a basket of food – full
of rice, lentils, peas, beans and so on – that would hopefully
last them until the next delivery. We also gave them a special ration of two kilogrammes of rice, two kilogrammes of
bulgur wheat, two kilogrammes of ghee, a bottle of corn oil
and fifteen packets of chicken soup.

After making sure we had enough food for everyone we
were helping, the next priority was to get better equipped
for our rescue work, including buying and equipping new
ambulances. We succeeded in getting a fleet of four cars
ready, using old vehicles that we adapted. Then, once we'd
finished preparing our ambulances and putting them into
service, we started to collect stray cats, especially from the
destroyed areas. These cats, like so many others, had been
abandoned because the inhabitants had emigrated when
the bombing became so bad. We were able to bring more

than a hundred cats, from all the areas of Aleppo, back to the sanctuary, and, if they were hurt or ill, we treated them and took care of them.

Of course the treatment we gave them was only as much as we could manage, depending on the amount of medicine we could find, as there was no vet who could help us. Most of the qualified people had left, and there were very few medical supplies for anyone, let alone cats. We did as much as was possible in the circumstances, and I drew on the experience I'd built up since childhood. I also took advice from my friends in the Facebook group. Some of them are vets themselves, so they were able to advise me on what to do when it was a more complicated case, and, by early 2015, we had managed to save around 170 cats in total. We kept them safe in our sanctuary, our special cats' house, Ernesto's Cat Sanctuary.

People in Aleppo were rather taken aback by what we were doing and everything that had happened. No one could imagine that, thanks to the cats, people had received help too, using me and my love of cats as the channel for it. They thought I was just a crazy person who loved cats and they couldn't quite grasp how me helping cats was now also helping them.

In the beginning we started with the poorest families in our community. For example, we helped people whose children needed to have operations because they'd been injured in the bombing or were sick, and offered to cover the costs of these operations, and so they went to Turkey at the expense of our group in order to continue their treatment. Then there would be the cost of the medicines afterwards to cover, so we also bought medicines for people who had chronic diseases and who needed regular medication but couldn't afford it. We helped many elderly people as well as children in this way.

The other thing we started was an awareness campaign about cats. We wanted to raise children's awareness about the welfare of their pets, and how they should take care of them. I was able to sow the seeds of love and mercy towards animals and people in children's hearts, to help them feel compassion for the suffering of others. The awareness campaign was very successful, I'm glad to say, and so many children responded, even though this was all happening during the fighting and bombing in Aleppo. Many people might think that looking after animals was the last thing to be worried about, given what was going on, but we found that the children needed the distraction very much.

At the beginning, people often criticized me and my work, as they simply didn't understand what we were doing. People here are suspicious of cats. They think cats are ungrateful, just because they close their eyes when they eat, as if they don't care about the person who feeds them, while dogs somehow seem to show more gratitude and loyalty to the person who gives them their food. Cats can be beautiful, affectionate, agile and strong, but they can also be crafty, unpredictable, thieving and cruel. Some cats will steal food, and the cat's owner in Islamic law is responsible for any loss caused. People feel they are ambiguous creatures, and black cats especially are seen as mischief-makers and even a cause of broken friendships. So you can imagine the stigma I had to overcome when explaining my work. But I told them: 'These animals have no one to help them. All the people who used to look after them have left the country and emigrated. These animals need our help. They're like poor and vulnerable people who couldn't leave the country and who've lost their homes'.

Slowly, once they began to understand that the purpose of the sanctuary was to help people in need and to establish the first ambulance system, as well as help cats, they started to see it differently.

*

When I'd been working with Syria Charity before I'd met Alessandra, I didn't feel I could have cats with me in the ambulance, because their charity was only about rescuing people. If I came across a cat that needed rescuing, I would have to leave it, because I felt I couldn't take it into the Syria Charity ambulance. However, when my Facebook friends at Il Gattaro d'Aleppo raised the money for me to buy my own ambulance, I felt free to take cats with me and to rescue any animals I found in the lulls between my work rescuing people.

It also gave me the freedom to go where I wanted to do this rescue work. Sometimes I wanted to go to places that were far away, even if it seemed as if there'd been no victims in the areas being bombed. I was keen to do this, as it often happened that, when I went to an area where nobody expected there to be victims, or where rescuers had already been and taken away some injured people, there were still more people left behind, hidden under the rubble somewhere.

Once, I went to a place that had been bombed in the Old City of Aleppo. The Civil Defence White Helmets had finished their rescue and thought there was no one left at the bombed site. I was nearby at the field hospital, Shawqi Hilal, where the casualties had been brought, and there was a family asking about a little girl, their daughter. They were asking if anyone had rescued her from their destroyed house and they were going around all the hospitals looking for her.

So I returned to the bombed site and asked any neighbours I could find, in case she was with them. I searched the whole area, thinking maybe she was injured and unable to make a sound, which was why nobody had noticed her. And sometimes during bombardment children are physically thrown great distances by the blast. Often we found bodies on the roofs of buildings which hadn't even been bombed.

Thankfully, I found the girl hiding under a staircase. She was only six years old and she'd been unable to call out or scream because she was paralysed with fear and in a state of shock. Her eyes were open but she couldn't talk. The rescue team had been in the building for about forty-five minutes, rescuing other people from the rubble, but they hadn't noticed her. I took her to the hospital, where they circulated the news that she'd been found to all the hospitals in the area. Her family heard the news and came to take her away, thank God. They took her and left Aleppo, so I don't know what happened with her after that.

A similar case to this appeared on the BBC – a little girl who had been left behind after the Civil Defence rescue team had left for the hospital with the other casualties, thinking they'd swept the site of all the injured. I was there too and I'd taken her brother and sister to Al-Sakhoor Hospital, before returning to look for more victims. I found her lying in the street. You could barely see her – she was so covered in dust that she was the same colour as the stones. Someone took a video of her in the ambulance, which is what the BBC showed. Shrapnel had penetrated her liver, her mouth was injured and her arm was broken, but she was unconscious and didn't feel anything. Afterwards I followed up her case and took her to the cat sanctuary and to the playground we had built alongside it, where she spent some time laughing again, which was good to see.

★

As well as levelling the ground and planting more trees at the sanctuary, we also planted trees in front of people's houses and in the neighbourhood generally. There was still a plant nursery selling trees and flowers at that time, the last one left in Aleppo, run by a man nicknamed Abu Ward, which is Arabic for 'Father of the Roses'. We also did other things to help improve life for people, like removing excess sand and rubbish, with the help of other workers, and renovating houses that had been bombed. When a wall had been destroyed, or a house had lost its ceiling, we repaired it to make it habitable again, especially during winter, when it was often very cold at night. And we also helped other groups, such as the Civil Defence White Helmets, who, like us, were rescuing people that had become trapped under the rubble and the collapsed buildings. We helped them by providing them with foodstuffs and we supported them a lot by helping them fix their own ambulances.

*

I was particularly pleased whenever the children asked their parents to bring them to the kids' playground alongside the sanctuary, which we built thanks to our donations from abroad. The children would ask their schools to bring them too. So then the schools from the neighbourhood began to come on trips to the playground and the cat sanctuary. The playground was right next door to the cat sanctuary, so it was easy for them to enjoy both at the same time.

In the playground we had lots of special equipment to play on, which had been donated by people like Nicoletta, Lorraine and Simona, who are in the Facebook group. My friend Nicoletta, for example, gave a really generous donation to buy a wonderful ship swing for the children to play on. This ship swing is our favourite thing in all Aleppo. We call it 'the big ship', as it's a huge model that swings to and fro and goes very high, and lots of children can ride in it together. The children were so happy – the playground was still outside of the war zone at that time, so the children and their families could escape for a time from the constant fear that they usually had to live under.

We also took care of orphans via the sanctuary, as well as organizing special events for children. My Facebook friends had the idea of celebrating children's birthdays, so on any local child's birthday, we used to have a party for all the children at the sanctuary or maybe their school, with a big cake, juice and toys. All of this was funded by our generous Facebook friends. It was such satisfying work. We were able to offer so much happiness and joy to these children whose lives had been turned upside down. All they'd known in this crisis till then had been chaos and confusion.

As time went on, we held more than 500 birthday parties a year in this way, using the donations from my friends in the group. We continued to throw these children's parties even during the toughest times, when the warplanes were bombing very close to us. Thank God we were able to protect them and to help them escape, even if for only a short time, from the fear and horror that they lived with in their daily lives.

As well as the birthday parties and the school trips for children, we also helped other places, like old peoples' homes, via the sanctuary. There was one for Christians, for example, and we regularly gave them foodstuffs and medicines, as well as holding parties and celebrating special occasions with them, like Easter. The home was called Mar Elias, and it was located in Al-Jdaideh, in Tananeer Square. These Christians had remained in Aleppo. They didn't leave us. They said they preferred to stay, in solidarity with the oppressed people. We visited them regularly, and we talked and laughed a lot together. We even used to visit their church, and they liked to explain everything and show us their icons, or holy pictures, and the relics, which are all very precious to them. I could see that they were lonely and they always wanted us to come more often and suggested we visit them on Fridays, as they assumed we had the day off then for the Muslim holy day, but we explained that while we would've loved to visit them more often, we had to work day and night with no holiday at all in these difficult times. I think they understood, but they still kept asking.

Most of the residents in the home were women and there was one called Maggie, who'd been the chief nurse at

Kalemeh Hospital in Aleppo, which was an excellent hospital with very professional staff. She was about eighty-five when I first met her and she showed us black and white photos of herself as a young woman, looking very beautiful. We used to joke with her about how she should maybe marry a young man on our team, who was very handsome and whom she liked a lot. We flirted and laughed with her like this to make her feel young again. I felt sorry for her because she didn't have anyone else; most of her family had either left or died.

During Ramadan, we often shared *iftaar*, the special meal to break the fast at the end of the day, with them. Sometimes we took it straight to them at their home; sometimes, if there was time, we prepared *iftaar* with them at Mar Elias and then we all ate together. They had a real respect for Islam and for us and knew lots of Islamic expressions. We were so happy. And my friends in the Facebook group helped us provide them with many things, like the special lights that we installed because they were old and couldn't see well. Then, when a shell destroyed part of their building (their location in Tananeer Square, near the citadel, was close to the front line), four or five families, local residents who were Muslim, helped repair the damage for them. People helped each other, regardless of religion.

We also helped the Muslim old peoples' home, which was called Dar Al Salam, located in Al Mouyaser Square. We used to visit them and give them clothes and foodstuffs too.

At one point, we gave them 3,000 euros' worth of food, to help them during the siege – we brought them lots of tinned food that they could keep as stores in order to survive. And, we installed lights for them as well, so that they could see and move around after dark when there was no electricity. We even bought a radio for them to listen to, and the batteries for it to run off. We helped them in the same way as we helped the Christian old people's home. They liked us a lot and they were very happy when they learned that it was a cat sanctuary that was helping them, and offering them these things. It was very beautiful work.

*

Throughout all this time, as our projects were growing and developing, my special cat, Ernesto, was my constant companion. Whenever I'd been out helping people, Ernesto was always there waiting for me when I got home. For me, Ernesto was like a good omen. There's an old saying that goes: 'My sorrows will be over when I find companionship in a cat', and Ernesto had been with me from the very beginning, when I first met the friends from the Facebook group and when I first received the funds to help people in our neighbourhood. I remembered what my grandparents always taught me, that cats bring good luck. They also taught me that, when cats eat, they pray to God to help the person who's feeding them and to bring them good fortune. I really believe this.

The Cat Man of Aleppo

Ernesto and the cats of the sanctuary have all sorts of fans in the Facebook group Alessandra set up, and among them there are singers and artists, TV presenters and journalists, painters, and other famous people from around the world. I've got to know many, many people through these cats, and there's a lot of love among us. They are all so very compassionate and merciful, with big hearts, these friends, and they come from Britain, Italy, Germany, Sweden, Poland and Belgium, and from all sorts of other countries all around the world. They all have lots of questions about the sanctuary and our work, and they want to know every detail, which often means that they message me all the time. If I'm late and I don't communicate with them, they worry and message again. They stand by me and they care about the innocent lives who are in such danger. It's been a great thing, what we've all achieved together, with the cooperation and support from people of all religions, of all nationalities, and from all around the world. This cat sanctuary we built together was the first sanctuary of this kind, not just in Aleppo, but in all of Syria; in all of the Middle East.

6: Jihadis

Al-Baghdadi was a big cat with long hair, black and white in colour. He first came to the cat sanctuary alone. He just walked in, all by himself, to get some food, and from then on he used to come regularly to eat. I called him Al-Baghdadi after the leader of ISIS, because he was evil, in looks and in behaviour, especially at dinnertime.

Most of the cats were familiar with the routine of when food would be given to them, so they would gather at the appropriate time. When I was getting ready to serve the food at the appointed hour, however, Al-Baghdadi would stand a short distance away watching me, then, as the other cats came forward to eat, he would pounce. He would beat up the other cats, pushing them away from the food to make sure he got there first. After that he would either take the food away somewhere else to eat it or would devour it on the spot, with all the other cats keeping their distance. He always made a weird loud sound while he was eating, which made the others avoid him even more. Although Al-Baghdadi, our extremist cat, was very aggressive with the other cats, I couldn't throw him out. I gave him food, but I found a solution where I put his food a bit further away, in order to keep him away from the other cats.

Of course, this cat was a million times better than that evil murderer Al-Baghdadi, but this name had come to mind because his presence in the sanctuary coincided with the arrival of ISIS gangs in Aleppo. It all began in early 2013, when the group called Jabhat Al-Nusra first appeared in the city. They were an extremist jihadi group who had been linked with Al-Qaeda, but then they had split into two groups – Al-Nusra and ISIS. But ISIS didn't stay long in Aleppo, thankfully, because ordinary people fought against them, kicking them out after only a few days and forcing them into the countryside outside the city. They were made to leave because no one supported them, and so they moved to Al-Bab instead, a town an hour's drive away to the north-east. Later, ISIS was kicked out of Al-Bab as well, and now Turkey controls the town and the countryside around it.

It was the Americans who had made the fundamental mistake of releasing Al-Baghdadi from the Abu Ghraib prison, near Baghdad, in 2004, a year after they had made the even greater mistake of invading Iraq to begin with. He then joined up with other Islamist extremists released in 2011 from Syria's Saydnaya Prison, near Damascus. But while the Americans let Al-Baghdadi and others out thinking they were harmless, people believed that Assad let out several hundred Islamists from Saydnaya on purpose, knowing they would go off and cause trouble. The regime even helped them get started, so the rumours ran, giving them money and weapons. That way, Assad calculated, he could justify his claim that he was killing 'terrorists' to the outside world, when people started protesting about his violent crackdown on protesters – even though it was thanks to him that these people were at large to begin with. But even Assad didn't expect them to grow into the power-house they later became, funded by outside money and extortion, beheading 'non-believers' in front of the world's media: they were like a Frankenstein monster that grew out of control.

In what had begun as the Syrian revolution, these Isla-mist jihadi groups became a big problem. The first fighters against the regime had been what we call *Al-Jaysh Al-Hurr*, the Free Syrian Army. They were a group of defectors from all ranks who really wanted to get rid of the regime. But soon they were joined by lots of other groups, who were much more religious. Most Syrians follow a moderate kind of Islam, which is open and tolerant of non-Muslims. But these jihadis were people with a different ideology to us. They wanted to overthrow the Assad regime, not because it was corrupt and brutal, but because it was 'godless'. They wanted to replace it with an Islamist regime, one that was just as corrupt and brutal as Assad's regime.

Most of the jihadi groups that started to appear inside Syria from 2012 onwards were not even from Syria. In the

Saif Al-Dawla area of Aleppo in that first summer of 2012, I saw Muslim fighters from Saudi Arabia, Algeria, Senegal and Pakistan. Some of the rebels welcomed them and said they were good fighters who were not afraid. Others said they were frightened these foreigners would bring trouble. 'We've enough headaches already,' they said.

We all knew that Al-Baghdadi was an evil man, claiming to be the new caliph of what he called the 'Islamic State' – our word for this group, *Daesh*, comes from the Arabic initials of 'The Islamic State of Iraq and Syria', just like the English 'ISIS'. But we don't consider the followers of ISIS to be true followers of Islam. True Muslims accept all religions and people. ISIS doesn't understand Islam at all; they just pretend they are religious.

I'm not an expert in religion either, mind you; I leave all that to those who have studied it properly. I don't even consider myself a particularly religious man, but I'm a Muslim who follows the steps of Islam as much as I can, because I feel religion guides us to the right path in life and I get many good things from my religion.

I respect all other religions too. We have a lot of Christians in Aleppo, about 15 per cent of the city, although it used to be one third Christian a hundred years ago. Jews used to count for about 7 per cent, but now there are almost none. The communities have become even smaller during this war, so no one knows for sure how many are left now. I've read a lot about Christianity and Judaism and have found that there's much to learn from them. We all believe in the same God, and I respect all prophets who received messages from God to convey to the people. I believe in Moses, Jesus *and* Muhammad, because all of them had a noble aim. I'm a Muslim, but I am not a fanatic. I just take from religion everything that's good and that I can learn things from.

Thanks to the Facebook group, I now have friends from around the world with different beliefs, including Christians, Jews, Buddhists and so on. None of them want to hurt me and I don't want to hurt them. We all know our God and our way of life, and we know what we must do in life to help people. Religion must guide us to do good works and show us how to be kind and considerate to others. This should be the character of any believer, to be good to others and cause no harm. It is important to me that, above all else, I do not care about religion as much as I care about people.

★

One day in Aleppo, a group of Jabhat Al-Nusra fighters stopped me in the street. They wanted to challenge me because they knew that many of my friends are foreigners and Christians.

'You are a *kaafir*, an unbeliever,' said one of the fighters.

'Why do you say that?'

'Because you are talking to Christian Crusaders who are killing us.'

'But they're not killing us.' I replied. 'We're fighting a dictator, so it's nothing to do with Christians.'

'The Christians are supporting the regime.'

I knew I was risking a lot by confronting them, but I wanted them to understand. So I explained: 'In the Christian areas the regime is in control, so they have no choice but to submit to the regime. Go and stay in their area and they will support you instead. They like humanity and they're against any kind of fighting. They're not responsible for what their governments are doing, so please don't talk about religion when you speak about my humanitarian works, or when you speak about my friends, whether they are Christians, Jewish or foreigners of any kind. Keep religion out of it and don't say that I am an unbeliever in Islam.'

I then told these Jabhat Al-Nusra fighters a story about something that happened with my friend, who happens to be Polish. I had organized a party for orphans in Aleppo, in the Saladin quarter. I posted a video afterwards showing the party, and this Polish friend was so happy about what I'd done with the orphans that she commented on the video, writing: 'Muhammad really is a great person.'

My first name is actually Muhammad, so I thought maybe she meant me, but when we continued the conversation, she told me that she meant our Prophet Muhammad. She then went on to tell me all sorts of stories about him that I didn't even know. I said to myself, 'I think she knows more about our Prophet than I do, yet she's Christian and I'm Muslim. She's read about the Prophet Muhammad and how great he was, and how he had sympathy for all humankind and for all different religions. She knows many stories about him, how he was merciful even with his enemy.'

I ended my conversation with the people from Jabhat Al-Nusra by saying: 'Our Prophet Muhammad was good to everybody. He spoke with all Christians and Jews. How will people be able to like Muslims if we behave like you behave? We should be kind and merciful with others. God is the one who decides who is good and who is bad. It's not for us to decide. I know exactly how I worship my God. I know how to pray, between me and Him. It's not for you to judge me and to say I am a non-believer. Leave me with my friends, whoever they are.'

I strongly believe that conservative people who falsely present themselves as religious people are bad. A truly religious person should be moderate. If you see somebody who's making a mistake, you may advise him, but then you should leave him to decide what to do and how to behave. It's not our business to control the behaviour of others. One of the punishments these extremists use is to whip people who go against what they think is right. This could be for something as minor as a man talking to his girlfriend. Isn't that sad?

I wish that those people in Syria fighting to control areas

of the country were religious in a proper way, because, if they were following Islam in the *right* way, and following in the Prophet's footsteps and doing as God instructs, they would be merciful and tolerant with everyone. Unfortunately, their religion is a facade. People have allowed the message of the different holy books to become confused, but these holy books all tell us how to live in peace. God created us to live happy lives, and to stand with each other, not to fight or to force people to believe as we believe. Some jihadi extremists even say: 'I swear by God that I will never leave a Christian alive. Either I will kill him or I will die!' These people are evil and not Muslims at all. They are the ones who are *kaafirs*, unbelievers.

Our Prophet Muhammad said: 'Destroying the Kaaba [this is what we call our holy shrine in Mecca, which we pray towards every day] is a thousand times less harmful than killing one Muslim.' Imagine how important the Kaaba is for Muslims, but a human being is more important. It's forbidden in Islam to kill anybody, not just a Muslim. You cannot end the life of someone just because of his religion. God created us and it is not for people to destroy God's creation. In ancient times they used to kill a murderer when he killed an innocent person, but we live in modern times now and there are laws controlling all of this. We have prisons to punish murderers. It's not permitted to kill people just because they're Christian or Jewish. But, in reality, religion is nothing to do with what these extremist groups are saying. If they understood the teachings properly, they wouldn't kill.

I believe that all religions are based on love and humanity. And everything that we're witnessing now is not because of any religious issue; it's a purely political issue. Through funding terrorist groups and providing them with weapons, and then creating a sectarian conflict, the main aim of so many of those driving all this has been to destroy a country. Fundamentally, it's all about selling weapons and making fortunes.

Of course people have used religion as an excuse for war for a long time. Syrian politicians have long used religion in politics, often pretending to be religious themselves, and this spreads sectarianism. I hate it when politics involves religion and when religion involves politics. I believe that church and state must be separate from each other and that politicians should leave religion alone.

Yet, in any country, when the regime fails or is in danger of collapse, that failing regime will often use religion to defend itself, stirring up conflicts between the different sects, in order to make them fight and create a diversion, which can then lead to a civil war. They tell the pro-regime people that the others will kill them if they don't kill them first and so it begins. But, in Islam, the Prophet Muhammad said: 'You have your religion and I have mine', which means that everyone is free to practise his own beliefs. I strongly believe in this. I believe that it's governments that create hatred, which they then spread among people in order to control them. The majority of the fighting in the Arab world is because of sectarianism, which I don't support at all.

Most wars in the world are built on religious reasons, not just in Syria. We've learnt a lot of hard truths from these seven years of war. For example, before the war I used to think that the jihadis were good Muslims who understood more about Islam than me. Not anymore. Now that I've seen how these jihadis behave and what they've done in Syria, I realize I was wrong. I believe that a true jihadi should first protect his family, then fight for his land and for innocent people. Being a jihadi is nothing to do with fighting for a sect or a religion. People now hate each other in a way that they didn't before, thanks to these militants who misuse religion. I pray with all my heart that all of this ends soon and that Syria can return to what it used to be.

*

One thing that made me particularly angry and upset was to see how ISIS and the jihadis started to use cats in their recruiting propaganda. I don't know if they were maybe copying me, or whether they were just taking advantage of the internet's ongoing mania for cat videos to attract potential jihadis into their networks. 'Cats of Jihad' became a trendy thing for them, and they posted pictures on their social media accounts of kittens with rifles, looking cute.

The videos showed cats playing with guns and jihadis handing out sweets to children and eating Nutella, and also jihadis playing with a kitten with one hand and with an AK47 rifle in the other hand. It was all part of them trying to portray jihadis as nice, normal people, but it was really evil.

They even had Twitter accounts with names like @ISILCats and @TheIslamicStateOfCats, to try to give the impression that it was normal to go and fight in Iraq and Syria, and that everyone had pet cats in their new 'Islamic State', just as they did back in Europe and elsewhere. They wanted to normalize the concept of life as a jihadi, and I'm sorry to say it worked for a lot of people. They sometimes called the cats 'mewjahids', as a pun on the Arabic word 'mujahids', which means people who fight in jihad, and then showed kittens playing alongside bodybuilding weights, guns and ammunition. They were very clever to use cats like this, but very evil.

★

When the bombardment intensified in Aleppo, our extremist cat Al-Baghdadi ran away, just as ISIS had. We didn't even have to drive him out, as we had done with ISIS, because, like most other cats, even big tough ones, he was scared of loud noises and explosions. Cats have very sensitive hearing, among the best of any animal – they can hear sounds that are very faint and that we cannot hear at all, so the bombing for them is even worse than it is for us, even more frightening. I don't know what happened to our extremist cat Al-Baghdadi after he left us, but I would forgive him and feed him again if he re-appeared. If we treated him well, in the true spirit of Islam, maybe he would have learned to behave better in the end.

7: A Failed War

The boy was in shock, calling out his sister's name, looking for her. He was screaming and crying: 'Asmaa!' In his hand was a sandwich, but there was shrapnel in the sandwich. When his home had been blown apart, he had been thrown clear of the building and into the street, and yet he never let go of the sandwich. In the video of him taken at the time, he's moving the sandwich from one hand to the other. This sandwich probably saved him. If it hadn't been for the sandwich, the shrapnel might have penetrated his body. I took the sandwich and put it aside to wash his face.

Horribly, we then found his sister's body on the ground, but we couldn't find her head. There had been a shop in front of the children's house and, due to the heavy shelling, the wall had been blown off, scattering the family far and wide. This was in Hanano, in an area where the houses were old but not very strong. We eventually found Asmaa's head high up on the shop sign, so we took it down and gently laid it with her body in the ambulance. We washed her face too, as we had her brother's, which was when she briefly opened her eyes. I don't understand how this could be, but I swear by God that it happened.

I then told Asmaa's father and brother: 'Let's take her to the hospital.' She was wearing red and was only one year old, the poor child. The father carried his little girl in his arms all the way, sitting next to his son. The video of them I mentioned was made by a photographer from the Aleppo Media Centre, and it went on to be circulated widely, which helped the boy and his family, who had clearly been through so much, to receive a lot of support from people who viewed it. I don't know which country they are in now, but I hope they are safe. This incident, which has stayed with me, happened at the start of the barrel bombing campaign in Aleppo, in 2016, but, in actual fact, there wasn't much heavy shelling at that time. It was at the very beginning, before there were many casualties. This family was among the early victims. It was heart rending, the video the photographer captured, and, while he was filming it, I said to him: 'This piece you are filming will last forever. It will be historical. It will immortalize our struggle.' I will never forget that day.

★

When I think back to before the war, we used to be so shocked if we saw blood on the ground. But then, once the war was underway, we often saw blood and the remains of people and it became ordinary. Once, early on, I dug out from the ground the remains of a man who had been buried in the rubble, but as rescue work was new to me at that time, I was afraid to see his blood and got dizzy and nearly fainted. I can hardly believe that now, looking back – I've had to become hardened to such sights. Now, because of working in ambulance and rescue, I have learnt to move and act quickly. This, I found, helped me to avoid drops in blood pressure, brought on by the shock of all the horrific things I saw, and stopped me from passing out. If I looked at blood when I was standing still, I used to faint. But now that I've learnt to control this reaction, I've gone on to rescue thousands of people during these last seven years, always moving fast, and never fainting once. Those years of rescue work sometimes feel equivalent to seventy years not seven, because they have been so very tough. But I really don't care about myself; I care about children and animals, because both need the help of people like me, and the others who also do this work. They need us. Children and animals are the big losers in the Syrian war, when it's the adults who so often behave badly.

The war in Syria is extremely harsh. As far as I know, nothing on this scale has ever happened in any other Arab country. It is such an ugly war, and none of the factions, including the regime and the opposition, have done any good for people. They are all responsible – the regime, the opposition, and all the others who've piled in – for what has happened.

A Failed War

At the beginning it was a peaceful revolution, then it turned into a fight, thanks to the intervention of other countries. Those countries are equally responsible for this ugly war. When Bashar al-Assad made his claims about there being a conspiracy against Syria, he forgot to say that this conspiracy is actually against the Syrian people, and that he's a part of it. So many civilians have been killed because of the fighting between the regime and the opposition, and the opposition's militant groups fighting among each other. I blame *all* fighting parties equally, no matter who they are or why they say they're fighting, for the killing of civilians.

Most of Aleppo city, and in particular the old part of the city, has been destroyed because of this war. The rebels, when they chose to take up arms, should have fought the regime in the less populated regions, away from the built-up areas where people lived, or, alternatively, at the regime's military bases, which are all over the country. They should have fought there until the regime was toppled, not in the poor neighbourhoods where people didn't have any choice or way to escape. They hurt those people by entering their areas, far more than the people they claimed to be fighting. I think the revolution was doomed to failure as soon as the rebels entered the cities. The Syrian regime doesn't care about civilians: they simply bombed and destroyed and burned all the areas that got out of their control.

In my opinion, what has happened in Syria is a failed

war. The opposition groups say they're seeking democracy and freedom through this fight, and the regime is fighting to defend its reign and stay in power, but they are both big losers. And yet the biggest losers of all are always the civilians: civilians have lost their houses, their businesses, their families and their children. So many children have lost their parents and now there are so many people who have been injured and disabled by this war, more than three million of them. Syria is a tragedy. Never did I think I'd live to see Syria in this state.

Another fallout from the war has been the quarrels within families. Because of the war, people started to argue about things they'd never discussed before. They started to question each other's points of view and not just accept things like they used to. The divorce rate really shot up; it used to be very low, with only about 2 per cent of our marriages ending in divorce, but now it's skyrocketed. It's a new thing in Syria. Time will tell what impact it will have long term, I suppose, but I worry about the children, who are the ones most affected when their homes are broken and their parents live in different places.

*

My wife and children left Aleppo at the point when the bombardment had begun to intensify along the Castello Road. By then, in late 2015, the Russians had entered the war on the side of the Syrian regime and they had started to carry out airstrikes on east Aleppo. Everyone knew that the regime, with the help of the Russians, was trying to block the Castello Road, which was the only road into the area on that side of the city. Everything passed along it – humanitarian aid, fuel, foodstuff, medicines. For two months, my wife had been saying she wanted to leave and take the children to safety in Turkey, where she had family living in Istanbul. She knew that my rescue work meant that I could not leave, but she had no one else in Aleppo anymore. Her family in Istanbul kept telling her she should leave before Aleppo got locked down, and that lots of other families were leaving, which was true.

The only way out, however, was along the Castello Road. I knew how dangerous it was, and I was extremely worried that they would be targeted not only by the regime but also by the PKK Kurds and by thieves. The regime and the Kurds were working together at that time, targeting the civilians who were leaving Aleppo, because they assumed they were the families of the Free Syrian Army rebels. The thieves, meanwhile, were not linked to anyone, but were just greedy people who wanted to steal whatever they could, since the people fleeing the city were often taking with them everything of value they owned. It was a thieves' bonanza.

We generally advised individuals and families not to attempt to leave, because so many were injured, often fatally, in the attempt. We used to wait at Al-Jandool Roundabout so that we were close at hand to help rescue them when, inevitably, they were hurt. But, before the escaping families could head out onto the Castello Road, they had to pass the Youth Housing Complex, which was still under construction. The unfinished buildings there were occupied by the Kurds, and they used to shoot at the civilians in order to force them to remain under the siege, or simply to injure them. I saw it with my own eyes.

So, understandably, I was extremely hesitant to let them travel through all these dangers on the Castello Road, but my wife told me that she was afraid something even worse would happen to them if they stayed in Aleppo, and that I was always out and busy with my work anyway. It was true, but I kept delaying their departure, trying to keep them safe in other ways. I used to move them from one place to another, according to where the bombing was, so we might move to my sister's house for a few days, for example, but then return home once the bombing of that area was over.

Then, one day, I was waiting near the Castello Road when a yellow taxi pulled up close to my ambulance and I saw my wife and children sitting in the back seat waving at me. My wife had just decided to do it that day. I was shocked, but I couldn't persuade her to stay. The realization hit me that they were really leaving, there and then, and I couldn't stop them. Instead, I drove behind them along the Castello Road, so that if something happened to them and they were targeted, I would be there to help them, or if we were all targeted, at least we would all die together.

A Failed War

The journey along the Castello Road was very slow, because there were so many big bomb craters, and so much shrapnel and lots of destroyed cars. Sometimes you had to drive off the road and onto the red soil dirt track in order to avoid the blocked sections. It was certainly impossible to drive fast, because the cars would have torn their tyres or damaged their chassis. After the shelling each day, the Civil Defence people would usually try to clear the road and repair it, to keep it open so that aid and food could come in, but on that day, it was almost as if there was no war. No one fired on us. We heard no shooting and we drove all the way out of Aleppo, through Kafr Hamra, Babees, Ma'ara and Bashantra, through remote villages in the eastern country-side, and a long way further on, until we reached the village where I live now. My family waited there, in that village, for two days, then I sent them off with people I know to be smuggled into Turkey. Thank God at that time the border procedures were not very strict.

When they had gone, I could hardly stand on my feet. I was devastated, but also relieved that they had left safely. I knew it was a wise decision and their choice of day had been a good one. A month and a half after they left, the building where they'd been living in Karm Al-Qaterji was hit in an airstrike and partially destroyed. The procedures on the Turkish border also became much stricter and many people were even killed by Turkish border guards while they were trying to smuggle themselves across. The Turks realized that large numbers of people would try to flee Aleppo once the siege began, so they closed the border completely.

After my family had reached Istanbul, and I knew that they were now safe and being looked after by my wife's family there, I threw myself into my work. Their absence gave me even more motivation to help people, because I wanted to make my staying behind worthwhile.

*

Sometimes, when I was rescuing people, the family of the injured people would attack us and push us away. I remember one time I received a call for help on my wireless radio: I was told there were injured people on the Castello Road, so I drove there to help. A lot of vehicles brought fuel in barrels into Aleppo along this road, and if they were hit, they would catch fire, of course, and the fuel would burn very fiercely. On this occasion, there was a man whose truck had been hit, and his wife, who was travelling with him, got trapped inside the truck and the clothes on her back caught fire. The radio report also told me that there was another car with an injured family, including children, nearby too, but we didn't know their exact situation or location, so I put the woman with the burnt back in my car and waited while two young men went on motorbikes to find the other family. I told them to bring the children first. But the husband of the woman with the burns couldn't understand why we should wait. He shouted at me: 'Move, move!' I told him that I couldn't leave until the men brought the children back with them on the motorbikes. The woman was in pain, but not in a dangerous condition – I could see it was only second-degree burns, so I knew she could wait. She would live. But if the children were badly injured and needed an ambulance, I had to be there. There was no other ambulance in the area.

So he tried to hit me. He even tried to take my ambulance and drive off in it with his wife. He tried to grab my keys, so I threw them away to stop him. I was so angry that he attacked me, but there were several times like this when I was in a dangerous situation, not because of the shelling or the bombardment, but because of desperate people behaving badly.

When the injured children we were waiting for arrived with the men on the motorbikes, I could see that their injuries were only slight, but they were very frightened. When they were delivered into my car, it was as if they'd been drowning but had now been rescued from the water. The windscreen of the car they were travelling in had been smashed by the shelling, and the glass had cut their faces and their shoulders, but they were only superficial injuries, thank God. I drove them to the hospital and their wounds were treated easily. I stayed with them until they were all treated, because they were children and all alone, and drove them home afterwards. The children were okay in the end, but I considered that day a particularly painful and upsetting one, thanks to that man who had attacked me when I was only doing what I could to help.

★

The impact of the war on society was huge. We witnessed so many changes, especially in people's behaviour and mentality. We saw people who helped each other, but we saw others who wronged each other, and some people became criminals.

I will tell you a story that will give you some idea of just how badly this war has damaged our society. It is a story about electricity, a subject I know a lot about, thanks to my previous work as an electrician. In Aleppo, we had electric power in the usual way from the state, but there were always power cuts, even before the war, so a lot of businesses and places like hotels had generators to cover the drop in power, which could last a while, especially in the summer months. During the war, initially the power continued to be supplied to the city as before, but, after three years, the normal supply with the regular outages began to get much worse, and eventually, from around the end of 2015, the power was cut off completely. And here is the reason.

Maybe the revolution was honest at the beginning, but, by the end, it just degenerated into a big stealing competition. All the cables and generators were stolen, often by people who pretended that they were from the Free Army, but who were actually transferring the generators to the regime areas and then selling them. One generator can provide 2,000 or even 5,000 houses with electricity, depending on its capacity. They are very expensive, so when they get stolen, we can't afford to buy another one. If we don't have these generators, we don't have electricity. It's as if someone has just taken our air away. They would steal them at night. They even stole the cables and took the copper out of them in order to sell it, so we had to use the iron wire rope that people normally used to hang out their washing instead. And, of course, whenever they stole the cables, these gangs of thieves would quickly relocate to another area, so that we couldn't trace them, but they had people who were always watching and waiting for when the areas around the remaining generators were empty and unmanned.

When the robberies first began in Aleppo, a sort of 'quartet' was formed by ISIS, Jabhat Al-Nusra, the Free Army battalions and the battalions from the northern countryside. They formed a commission that was supposed to regulate security and to prevent theft, and there was a group of shaikhs who took on the role of the police force. They called all this the 'Committee for the Promotion of Virtue and the Prevention of Vice' and it was supposed to respond to people's grievances. For example, if someone in the neighbourhood had a problem, he could complain to them, because there were no official police to go to instead.

The Last Sanctuary in Aleppo

In our neighbourhood we wanted to watch the thieves to check up on them and be observers of what they were actually doing, because there were people who said that the stolen electricity cables and the phone cables that were being dug out of the ground, as well as the generators, were passing through the road close to our neighbourhood. They were stealing from the main industrial zone of Aleppo, Shaikh Najjar, about ten kilometres north-east of the city, beyond the Aleppo ring road, where there were more than 40,000 factories. That area suffered heavily during the war and became a wasteland of gutted buildings. Lots of the factories were looted, and then the stolen goods were taken along the old Shaikh Najjar road, near our neighbourhood. These thieves were stealing from the Muslimieh area of the cement factory, where they dismantled everything, and entered the city from there.

So one day we took them by surprise. We came out suddenly from our neighbourhood and claimed that we were an armed group. We each carried a weapon, not to use against anyone but just so that we could protect ourselves. We decided to stand and block them on the road. We told them that we were a people's security group. We scared them, and even told them that we were part of Jabhat Al-Nusra. Most thieves were afraid of Jabhat Al-Nusra, because they knew that this extremist group would chop off the hands of any thief. So they ran away and left the trucks. Thank God there was no shooting. There were eleven vehicles in total. Usually they move together in a convoy.

When we searched their trucks, we found two stolen electric transformers inside. They also had electrical cables of the type that can only be used by the state. The cables had been cut, so they couldn't be used. If a cable is still in one piece, it's very expensive, so they'd cut it into pieces. This was because they wanted to pretend they weren't selling anything, that they were just transporting old pieces of cables, hoping that no one would notice the electric transformers.

The problem was, once we'd captured the transformers, we realized we didn't know who to give them to. There was no state, no regime, so we were worried in case we gave it to somebody who might sell it again, or steal it again. We couldn't keep the transformers with us, because then they would accuse us of stealing them instead. So we decided to give them to that Committee for the Promotion of Virtue and the Prevention of Vice, because we thought they were shaikhs and religious people who knew about God and who cared about people. We also heard that they had an electric engineer, a specialist, who used to work in the public sector and who was meant to be helping people, fixing their electrical problems.

So, we took the transformers to the shaikhs. We told them the full story, and they thanked us a lot. Their electrical engineer told us that the equipment would be used for the circuits in the Al-Shakhoor area, as they didn't have a similar circuit in their own areas. He told us: 'Do you know how many people need this circuit? It's a great thing that you've done.'

Imagine how happy I was! We were all very happy, happy that we were able to bring back to people what they'd lost. So we unloaded the power transformers, handed them over, and they wrote down a report in their file about them. But the next day I received a message from the cultural centre of the grouping of four, this kind of quartet, to go to see them. It turned out the cultural centre was nothing to do with the Commission for the Promotion of Virtue and Prevention of Vice – everyone is working separately, there's no coordination.

So I went to this cultural centre and met the man who had asked me there. He had a white beard and looked religious.

'Alaa, may God give you health,' he said. 'Thank you for what you've done. I've heard a lot of nice things about you. You are helping people.'

The cultural centre was in Hanano, so it was the same area as I lived in – that's why he'd heard about me, from people in the neighbourhood. I didn't know him personally.

He went on: 'Thank you for what you've done, but you have acted wrongly. You are civilians and you carried weapons and fought against others.'

I was taken aback and said to him: 'Do you care about those people, those thieves?'

His reaction made me realize that he did; that he was in league with the thieves himself and that I was now in deep trouble. 'Where did you take the electricity transformers?' he asked me. I understood then that he wanted to steal them back from us.

So I said: 'We gave back things that were stolen from the people. I gave them back to be reused by the people. How can that be considered theft? You should say instead that you wanted me to hand them over to you instead!'

'Exactly!' he replied. 'We are the biggest power here, and we are responsible for these issues, such as theft and security. We are the quartet. We are the power.'

'Maybe you are, but you couldn't catch the thieves, and you can't protect people. That's why I handed those transformers over to the Committee.'

He looked at me sternly. 'I will keep your ID with me until tomorrow, when the group of shaikhs will meet in the medical centre. Then they will decide what to do with you.'

'You mean they might arrest me?' I said in disbelief.

'No,' he replied, 'but they may ask you to get the transformers back from the Committee. A representative of ours will go with you to get the transformers back.'

He took my ID (every Syrian always has to carry an

identity card with them at all times) and I said to him in disgust: 'You do whatever you want to do. My conscience is clear.'

I knew that the Committee was supposed to be providing people with electricity and fixing all the broken lines and cables. Instead, they were collecting all the stolen stuff and selling it again to thieves at auction. The thieves themselves are never arrested, because all the thieves have weapons and they were fighting.

Thankfully, on the second day he brought me back my ID and no further action was taken. I think they solved it amongst each other. They probably realized it looked bad and said to each other: 'Maybe we shouldn't attract people's attention to us and what we are doing!' But I witnessed many stories like that; they did the same sorts of thing with iron and copper. All the people who were in important positions, and who were generally religious people too, were all corrupt and thieves, all because they wanted everything to be done under their control.

What I've just told you was far from funny, it was tragic. One thing that *was* funny, however, was the forklift truck that had to carry the electricity transformers in order to hand them over to the quartet. This forklift truck had been something that I'd had to arrange at my own expense. It was virtually impossible during the war to find a forklift truck anywhere, let alone with a cheap price, so I paid dearly for it. I then sat beside the forklift driver and we moved the two transformers.

'Will you sell me the big transformer?' asked the driver, as we moved along.

I looked at him in disbelief. 'This transformer isn't mine. I can't sell it to you.'

'Yes, I know. It's public property, that only the state can install.'

'In that case why did you ask me to sell it to you?' I laughed. 'OK, let's say it is mine, how much will you pay for it?' I just wanted to hear his answer, because as an electrician, I knew its real value.

He said: '250,000 Syrian pounds.'

'When I was working in industrial electricity, I saw that a factory would pay 3.5 million Syrian pounds for a transformer. It's very expensive. So how could I possibly sell it to you for this price?'

The driver shrugged.

'And even if I *did* sell it to you, what would you do with it? Are you going to use it in your house?'

'No, I'll sell it to the regime.'

'How will you sell it to the regime?'

'There are people on the regime's checkpoints, and you pay them in order to reach the regime, then you sell it to them. There are merchants who're doing that. They're fighting alongside the regime. They're the groups who man the regime checkpoints, like the National Defence Forces and the *Shabiha* (the regime's Alawi militias). They're the ones who'll buy these items. I'll buy it from you, then I'll sell it to them.'

It was completely absurd.

'Ok, that's wonderful,' I said. 'Those groups at the regime checkpoints will steal it in order to sell it to the regime, and meanwhile we're left without electricity! What a revolution we had!'

Then I told him the truth – that we'd already seized both transformers from thieves and that I was taking them to hand them over for free. He couldn't believe that. When we arrived at the school where we supposed to leave them, it was hard to put them inside the premises. So I told him to drive onto the pavement and to lift them over the school walls and put them inside the courtyard, so that they couldn't be stolen again. While he was lifting them, I started laughing at the craziness of it all. He saw me laughing, and he was upset. He thought I was planning to sell them or to hide them somewhere. I could tell he was saying to himself: 'That person isn't going to hand them over, he's going to sell them.' He was wrong, of course, but he just couldn't imagine that I wasn't going to sell them.

★

Sometimes I think you need to find the humour in these situations, even in tough circumstances. We all found ways to get through. For me, the cats were a huge comfort. Some came and went from our sanctuary – either because they were of an independent nature or because they got frightened by the fighting all around us and ran away. But others stayed with me throughout.

Al-Moghanieh was one of those. This particular cat walks like a top model, moving her hips from side to side. It's a funny thing about cats, the way they walk. It's very unusual, because they are the only mammals, apart from camels and giraffes, who walk that way. They move their two legs on one side together, then their two legs on the other side. When they run or trot, they go to the normal pattern of opposite legs, like other mammals, so it's only this way of walking that is special, and Al-Moghanieh does it in a very exaggerated way. One of my friends said to me, when the cat first appeared: 'Look at this cat. She stands and walks and sings like a top singer performing, as if she's famous.' So, when I suggested to the Facebook group that we call her 'Al-Moghanieh', which means 'the Lady Singer' in Arabic, the name seemed perfect for her.

Al-Moghanieh is a very calm cat, white and grey in colour, and she immediately adopted the life of the Ernesto Sanctuary. When I found her in an abandoned area, it was very soon after we'd established the sanctuary. I brought her back, together with her two kittens. It was June and very hot. She was ill and hungry, and looked very tired because of the heat. She drank a lot of water, which is very unusual for cats. They never drink water much, because they have an incredible in-built system for coping with heat and regulating their temperature, much better than ours. They can cope with temperatures of up to 52 degrees Celsius without water. A vet who later worked with us told me about this. He said it's because they have very efficient kidneys, which allow them to survive on meat alone, with little to no extra water. When they get too hot, he said, they slow down their blood flow to their skin, and even lose heat by evaporation through their mouths. So they're very well designed for heat control. We humans can only manage without water to 38 degrees. It's hard to tell when cats are thirsty, though, because they don't pant like dogs. So it shows how ill she must have been when she first came, because she drank so much. She then decided she liked our sanctuary, so she stayed with us.

She's been here in the sanctuary ever since. She never left, and her two kittens have grown up in the sanctuary too. Al-Moghanieh and her family seem to me like characters that will never change, no matter what happens or what fate throws at them. I noticed that, in war, some people change and some don't. Some people behave very differently to how they behaved before. It's as if they are thinking 'It doesn't matter now, I can do whatever I want, nobody can stop me, so I can take advantage of this. Everyone is too busy with the war to chase me or to punish me.' Some people think like this and other people think the opposite, that, now more than ever, they need to help

Mohammad 'Alaa' Aljaleel, creator of *Ernesto's Cat Sanctuary* in Aleppo.

When war broke out in his hometown, Alaa began working as an ambulance driver amid heavy shelling.

As news of Alaa's sanctuary spread worldwide, donations for his community flooded in.

Relaxing at the sanctuary; (*below*) a cat accompanying Alaa in his van.

Travelling with Firas; (*below*) shelling hits the sanctuary.

Building a new
sanctuary and
veterinary clinic
for cats, dogs,
monkeys, horses
and many more
animals.

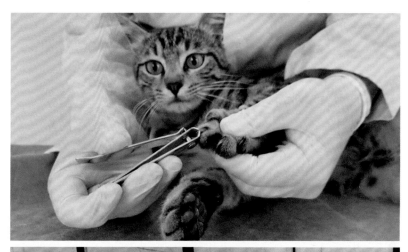

محمية القطط في سورية ـ منزل أرنستو

ilGattaro di Aleppo

The sanctuary provides a much-needed refuge for local children, with a playground and birthday parties; (*below*) Alaa pictured in February 2019.

people and stay together as a community. I think Al-Moghanieh would be one of those who would think like this. I think what happens in war is that the people who were always good before, stay good, but the people who only pretended to be good now feel free to show their true colours.

War is something very hard and tough. The true losers in war are always innocent civilians, mainly poor people, because rich people can use their money to flee or to travel or to buy food and to find a shelter. They can do many things to protect themselves.

We have a proverb that is similar to yours: 'When the cat is away, the mouse will play.' In Syria we use this when we talk about people who take advantage of someone else's weakness, so it has a negative meaning. It's saying that, if no one in authority is watching, people can do all sorts of things they wouldn't do normally. Maybe all the looting we had in Syria was a bit like this, when soldiers went into people's houses after an area had been evacuated and stole whatever they could, even right down to the electric cables and the window frames.

The war has affected the country very badly. So many people have become criminals. But it's not just Syrian criminals. Many other countries have got involved in it now. Every country claims that it's fighting against terrorism in Syria, including the United States, Israel, Turkey, Russia and the regime. But while they also say that they're fighting terrorism, the Iranians are, in fact, fighting against the Sunnis. I believe that Iran in particular has been the source of a lot of terrorism inside Syria.

But people survive as best they can. One man, a singer whose whole family was killed in the bombing, still carried on his singing, as he fed his pigeons on his roof. What else could he do?

No one wins in war, but we'll look after Al-Moghanieh and her kittens however long this war lasts. Like all of us, what she cares about most is her family. She does her best to look after them and we hope she succeeds in spite of this horrible war.

8: Final Warning

The man's car had been immobilized by shelling and was now sitting out in the open. He was vulnerable to sniper attacks, so I rushed out to rescue him. Luckily his injuries weren't too serious, just some shrapnel pieces in his arms and shoulders. I lifted him out of his car and into my van, now an ambulance, and drove him to the nearby field hospital improvised in a residential basement. All our hospitals in east Aleppo had been forced underground by the bombing.

He could still talk and wanted to tell me about the cargo he had with him in the car: a box full of mobile phones worth US$12,000. He told me he had a mobile phone shop where he planned to sell them.

'If you bring me the box,' he said to me, 'I'll give you $1,000.'

'You want me to die for mobile phones?' Now I'd heard it all. I couldn't believe it.

But he begged me. 'All my money is in those phones. Please bring me the box. It's money for orphans.'

I refused. I was sure it wasn't money for orphans and I told him thieves would probably have stolen the box by now anyway.

You could die on the Castello Road for many reasons. I would've died there to rescue a person or a cat, but not to rescue a boxful of mobile phones . . .

★

At that time we were being bombed by a lot of Sukhoi fighter jets. The Sukhoi is a very fast single-seater Russian plane. It's been around a long time, first appearing in 1981 in Afghanistan, in support of Soviet ground operations. They're old planes, but effective enough for the job required of them in Syria. Why waste more sophisticated planes when it wasn't necessary? There was never any threat to them, because the opposition didn't have any anti-aircraft weapons or any planes of their own. We always knew when the Russians were coming to bomb us because of their very loud engine noise. We'd shout: 'Watch out! A Sukhoi is coming!'

Sukhoi 25 also became the name of a cat I rescued from an abandoned and destroyed area. There was nobody else there at all, so he must have been through a lot of trauma from the bombing and noise and he was very hard to catch. I really had to coax him to trust me and let me take him home to Ernesto's cat sanctuary.

I monitored him for a few days, as I always do with any

new cat in the sanctuary. I noticed he was a very fast cat, especially when it came to getting his food. He ran very quickly, snatched the meat, then dashed away again to find an empty place where he could eat undisturbed. So, because of his style of running and his speed I called him Sukhoi 25, after the plane.

We also have another cat called Sukhoi 26. He's older than Sukhoi 25, and was an abandoned pet I found in the street. Sukhoi 26 is very sociable and likes people. He has a habit of standing on a wall and then launching himself about two metres through the air. His style of acrobatics is very rare and I've never seen another cat jump like this before. He particularly likes landing on my shoulders. We have lots of photos and videos of him doing this. He almost flies – I have many pictures of him 'flying' – so he deserves his name. The Sukhoi 26 plane, smaller than the older Sukhoi 25, was new in Syria at that time and bombed us a lot.

★

I often struggle to describe what I saw and lived through during those years. It's hard to understand how a government can bomb its own city and its own population. The siege of Stalingrad was in the Second World War and even I, who never studied properly at school, know that it was between two different countries, enemies who were at war, Russia and Germany. But here, in the siege of Aleppo, our own government sent their fighter jets, their Sukhois, to destroy us and our community. Their own people. Day and night we were bombed and what became clear was that we were their targets, ordinary people like me.

They bombed our houses, of course, but it was more than that – we started to see a pattern, targeting our way of life. During the quiet times, things in Aleppo were fairly normal. On these 'normal' days, when there was no shelling, people used to go out and go about their business. And even when there was some shelling, people would often still go out, to do their shopping, for example, to buy bread or vegetables. There were still functioning vegetable markets, and before the siege in 2016, we still got fresh vegetables from the countryside to the north. Life went on, but if an area close to the market was bombed, people would have to evacuate immediately, whatever they were in the middle of doing, until it was safe again.

So, one of the first things the regime and their Russian allies bombed was our markets and our bakeries. This was to make it impossible for us to go out and buy food. In Syria, the way we shop is through street markets, especially for fruit and vegetables. Supermarkets like you have in the West are not part of our culture, though one or two big ones appeared in the rich suburbs in the early 2000s, after Bashar Al-Assad came to power. The biggest shopping mall in all of Syria was the Chahba Mall, six kilometres north-west of the city centre, in the Layramoun District of Aleppo. It was built in 2008, to cater for the rich people in Aleppo and had five floors, with a big Carrefour supermarket in the basement and seven cinemas on the top floor. But ordinary people just went every day to the markets. The mall was used as a prison by the extremist groups during the war, as it happens, and then heavily bombed beyond repair in 2014. It's still closed now.

Bread is the other basic, the staple of our diet. Someone from every family goes to the bakery every day to buy fresh bread for the whole family. Usually it's the men, but sometimes a few women go too. You don't go inside the bakery. They're always just a small shop, with a simple hatch where people line up in the street to buy whatever quantity of bread the family needs for the day. If women go, our habit is to allow them to go to the front of the queue. We're brought up to respect women, especially mothers.

So thanks to the way we do our shopping, bombing the markets has always meant a lot of casualties, because so many people could be gathered there in the street. The regime deliberately chose the times when they knew the markets would be busiest, early morning and early evening. It was the same with the bakeries. They chose the mornings, when they knew the queues for bread would be longest. Imagine the chaos when people didn't return from going shopping. Shopping became a dangerous activity. You were a sitting target in the street markets and outside the bakeries.

We could understand the regime's logic in bombing these markets and bakeries once we thought about it. But we didn't imagine we would be targets even indoors, in places like schools and hospitals, places where people gather to be safe, to learn or to be looked after. Soon it became clear, though, that this was their way of thinking. If they bombed us in hospitals, it was their way of saying we couldn't escape them. Even if you were injured and had been rescued, they could still bomb you inside the hospitals. There was no escape, wherever people went, even places where you might imagine you would be safe.

Sometimes I would look up at the Sukhois and wonder what the pilots inside those jets were thinking. Did they think at all? Did they get some kind of pleasure from dropping their cluster bombs on us, knowing how many of us would be injured, disabled or killed? I couldn't understand how they were human at all. Yet these were my countrymen whenever the jets were Syrian. Only when they were Russian were they foreigners. That, I understood, might be different, more like Stalingrad perhaps. Except that it was not an equal fight. We were not equal enemies fighting each other on equal terms. They were in no danger from us. We had nothing to shoot them down with, and no planes to take them on in the skies. We were just like helpless ants below, awaiting our fate. No wonder the planes always seemed so casual, flying across the city in broad daylight, dropping their bombs and flying away again, knowing we were powerless to stop them.

The other pattern we saw was the 'double tap' bombing. After bombing any target, like a market, a school or a hospital, they would bomb it again a few minutes later, because they knew that, by then, rescuers would be there trying to save people trapped in the rubble. And many times I was one of those rescuers. I drove there in my ambulance and I would rescue people, often little children, and then take them as fast as possible to the makeshift underground clinics that people had improvised in the cellars and basements of residential houses, the only way we had of trying to escape the bombs.

*

I remember once there was an injured man from Helwanieh. His truck was on fire, so the Civil Defence people pulled him out. His clothes were on fire too, so they stopped the fire by smothering the flames with a blanket. They then put him in my car. Most of the time we didn't have any paramedics, so I had to improvise, and then be the driver at the same time. I was often alone, so had to do everything by myself. On arrival at the hospital, I had to carry people out of my car ambulance unaided and take them in. Imagine how difficult it was to do all this without anyone to help me.

The Civil Defence people had carried the injured man from Helwanieh to my ambulance car in the same blanket they had used to smother the flames. I then drove as fast as I could to the hospital. It was only about a minute or two away. The trip from Helwanieh Roundabout to Dar Al-Shifaa Hospital on the road to Al-Bab was a very quick one, because it was just along one straight street that crossed two areas. But I was driving so fast the air funnelled through my car in a strong draught through my open windows, and when I opened the back door to carry the poor man out, I found that the car was on fire because the blanket had caught alight again and the man was burning inside it. Maybe he was still on fire when they put him in the car, but they hadn't noticed, thinking the fire had been put out, or maybe when I drove so fast it fanned the flames and made him catch fire again? We faced so many problems like this during our rescue work. It was always difficult when we were under shelling, among the smoke and the dust and the fire, with so many people running and fleeing in panic. We had to make split second decisions.

When I arrived at the hospital the man was still alive, but dying. We usually never knew if people lived or died once we'd taken them to the hospital. Anyone who was injured and in a critical state was usually transferred immediately to Turkey, because we didn't have the equipment or the staff to carry out complicated and difficult operations. If the injury was minor, in the arms or legs for example, we expected people would survive.

Sometimes, if there was no ambulance to transfer them

to Turkey, or if there was a shortage, I would transfer them myself to the border at Bab Al-Hawa or at Bab Al-Salameh and deliver them there. I had to do that occasionally, but I always preferred to evacuate people and rescue them inside Aleppo if possible. I didn't like having to go out of the city, because of my responsibilities to the people of my neighbourhood and to the cat sanctuary. I worried about not making it back.

Sometimes, when we went to rescue people from a bombed area, there were animals needing to be rescued as well. They were victims too. On one occasion, the Civil Defence White Helmets helped me. They spent around forty-five minutes helping me get a cat out from under the rubble. It became a famous case, because there was a photographer there, who recorded it all. There were about six or seven people helping to get the cat out. It was howling and screeching with pain. We brought it to the sanctuary, where I put a splint on its broken thigh. It also had a big wound in its belly. I helped it in simple ways, because I couldn't take it to a hospital. When I brought it to the sanctuary, a paramedic friend and I did the stitches on its belly wound together. There were no vets, and the hospitals were full of human victims. They didn't have time for animals. Sadly, the cat lived just for three days.

We tried our best to save people and animals, whatever their situation was. A lot of the victims of the conflict by that point were old, people who felt they were too old to leave their homes. They just decided to stay put, no matter what. They were resigned to dying there. They were not on this side or that side. They found themselves caught up in this war not of their making and decided to see it through to the end, whatever that end might be. They were too old to start all over again somewhere else.

But the younger people, the ones with children who had to be looked after, but who didn't have the money to escape altogether, kept on having to start all over again. Each time their neighbourhood was bombed and they lost their home, they had to move again to a different part of the city. Then the bombing and fighting would catch up with them again. Some of them were forced to move many times.

Imagine what this did to children and their schools. Schools had become a target for the bombing too. I presume because the regime thought this was a good way of breaking our morale and spirit. If they killed the children, that would break the adults, and make them give up. After all this became too much of a pattern, a lot of parents decided to keep their children at home. They were afraid of sending them to school, afraid that they might never return. I remember going to so many schools that had been bombed, trying to rescue any children who were still trapped inside and underneath the rubble.

A lot of the more educated mothers, some of whom were teachers themselves, started to have schools in their own basements. Then the neighbourhood children only had to walk the short distance to the homemade school. Before the war, most children caught a school bus to get to school, but that became impossible now. Some families, who were in places where it was too risky even to go to a school close by, found other ways of coping, where the oldest child became the teacher for the younger ones, teaching them to read and write and do their sums. Who could imagine being a teacher aged nine or ten?

At the time we all thought it was temporary, that it would end soon. Surely the big international organizations like the UN would find a way of stopping the conflict? We knew that photographs and videos of the fighting and the war were being sent all round the world, so we assumed people would see what was happening and demand an end to the fighting. But no one did. The world just watched the videos and did nothing to help us. We were on our own.

As the bombing intensified, people learned how to be better prepared, to protect themselves. They even got monitoring devices, on which they could watch and observe the fighter jets. When they used these spying devices, they'd have advance notice, for example, if a military plane was flying towards the city. They'd be told: 'A jet just took off from T4 airport towards the north.' T4 is the regime's military airbase in the desert between Homs and Palmyra, their biggest airbase, so people knew, if it was heading north, it would arrive in Aleppo ten minutes later. So everyone had ten minutes to get off the streets and find a safe place to hide during the bombing.

We had plane spotters at fixed observation points and everyone had hand-held radios. You could get them in the shops, so everyone carried theirs whenever they went out in the street. Someone at the observation point would tell people that a military plane (Russian or regime) had just taken off from T4, say, or from Hmeimeem Airbase near Lattakia, and was heading towards Aleppo or the north. They would even try to identify where the military plane would bomb. Often, with a jet, that wasn't possible, but with a helicopter it was easier to work out the target.

For example, when the observer said on the radio that a helicopter had just taken off from the Defence Factories in Safira, twenty kilometres east of Aleppo – on bad days there were about a hundred take-offs a day from these defence factories – that observer would then ask all the other observers who were spread about everywhere, such as the Aleppo airport area, Bab An-Nayrab and other areas, to observe it and to see where exactly it was likely to enter Aleppo. Then it would appear like a giant buzzing bug, and they would watch it with binoculars so that they would know its direction. So, if people said on the radio: 'It's coming from Al Mouyaser area, flying towards Old Aleppo', people in that area and in the Old City who had these radios knew that the helicopter would soon be appearing above them, and they would leave the streets and hide in their houses. If there was a market, they evacuated it.

It was the same thing for military planes. The observers would say if it was flying to the north or the east, so we learned from experience exactly where they were going to bomb. We moved our ambulances according to this information. For example, if the plane came from the north and I was also coming from north, from Al Mouyaser, say, then I would worry that it would bomb near me, or even above me.

If I was coming from the north and the plane was coming from the east, however, then our paths would cross and I might find myself underneath it and be bombed. I tried as hard as I could to avoid being underneath a plane, as you can imagine. I used to watch out for them while I was driving, and I often hit rocks in the road, or even a wall once, because I was looking up and trying to watch a plane. But we learned to predict where the planes were going. We became experts.

The first year was hard, but then, once we had these radios and the plane spotters, we adapted. Just imagine, we knew that it would take three minutes for a helicopter to complete its turn and to return to the place of the first bombing, because on the hand-held wireless an observer was telling us: 'The helicopter's in the same axis and will bomb the same place. It didn't drop the two barrels at the same time. It just dropped one then it'll make its three minute circuit over the opposition areas, and then it'll return to the same place to drop the second bomb.' We also knew it would take thirty seconds for the barrel bomb to hit the ground. We could judge the time it would take to hit the ground according to the height of the helicopter, so, if we were in that area, we could hide until the barrel reached the ground. I benefited a lot as an ambulance man from all this knowledge. We learned a lot and quickly, and managed to protect ourselves and advise people.

★

When the barrel bombing campaign first began in Aleppo, in 2013, the regime used digit numbers as codes to identify their targets. At first we didn't know what these numbers meant, but gradually we learnt, thanks to the plane spotters, that the number 17, for example, meant the Ba'edin Roundabout. So we could warn people. But then the pilot saw that the area was already empty of people, so the regime realized that we understood their code.

After that, the regime stopped using the codes and just said things like: 'Go to the working area.' They bombed randomly. Sometimes the regime instructions to the pilot were just something like: 'Go to Bab An-Nayrab and drop two barrels on the same place or two places close to each other.' They stopped mentioning the actual target place. So the pilot just got his instructions about the direction and height, then he said: 'I'm ready to go', or 'I did it', or 'I'm near the target'. Sometimes they would tell him to go back or to do it again. We knew all this from our radio monitoring devices, which could intercept the regime's instructions and allow us to react quickly to protect ourselves, thank God.

One thing we couldn't protect ourselves from so easily was the phosphorus bombs. The Castello Road was very dark at night, so the regime would bomb it with phosphorus to improve visibility. This happened about a month before the siege began, because they didn't yet control the Castello Road. They were trying to close us off inside Aleppo by controlling it, because it was the only way we had to get in and out of the city. When they bombed us with phosphorus, it meant they could see all the vehicles and the land around the Castello Road. Lots of civilians were trying to leave at night at that time, using this road before the siege succeeded in trapping us, so there were lots of cars driving along it in the dark. The phosphorus lit up all the vehicle windscreens and the glass, and made it easy for people to be targeted. They were shot at from both sides, from the regime and from the PKK Kurds, because they were both monitoring the road at that time. During the day we used to hide our vehicles inside the factories or the warehouses so that they couldn't be seen. People from abroad warned us to keep away from the phosphorus, not to breathe in the white smoke. They told us it would hurt us, not in any obvious way straight away, like the chlorine gas, but later. They said it might affect our children. When they bombed with the phosphorus, the whole area was full of the white smoke that turned night into intense daylight.

*

I always kept a spare windscreen for my car to hand, especially during the siege. I always had a spare, because the first thing to be damaged was generally the windscreen, or the tyres. The tyres would be damaged by shrapnel and all kinds of metal – iron, aluminium – on the ground. We used to go to the bombed areas and there'd be shrapnel and metal everywhere, because the used shells broke into many pieces and scattered all over the ground. The tyres got shredded to pieces over and over, so I had to keep lots of spare tyres, as many as possible.

If it was the back windscreen that was broken, we would get a lot of very bad fumes coming into the car, which might hurt the injured person there. My car was a Hyundai minivan and, because the diesel we had was so filthy – it was very dirty fuel, dear God, not pure, because we could only get whatever fuel was available, however dirty it was – the car produced a lot of black smoke from the exhaust at the back.

Once I fixed my back windscreen because it had been smashed in a bomb blast and then drove straight to rescue people and take them to Al-Quds hospital. The area was bombed with cluster bombs and the new back windscreen got smashed yet again from the cluster blast sound. I'd only put it in an hour before, and it was the last one I had.

We suffered a lot because of these kinds of accidents, as well as from driving over potholes in the night. We always drove with our lights off, so that we couldn't be seen by aircraft machine guns, which would have shot at us if they'd seen us. They were always looking out for any moving light, such as car headlights. So there were more times than not when our windscreens were smashed and our tyres were shredded when we were moving at night in the dark.

★

Once I was hit by a car driving very fast, but thank God I survived. I was driving slowly but he was driving fast, and he hit me from the front. It was all because we were both driving with no lights on. I survived because the air bags opened and saved me. During all my work over five years in ambulance and rescue, I was never seriously injured or too psychologically affected, thank God. Shells often landed close to me or shots would just miss me. When I was first driving my ambulance, I was shot at on the airport road by a Type 23 machine gun. I saw the shots, which were red. Type 23s fire very big explosive shots. They explode as soon as they hit something, but if they don't hit anything, they explode anyway before they land on the ground. Maybe you've never seen these kinds of shots. None of us had seen them before the war, but we got to know many different kinds of weapons – Types 23, 12.5, 13.5 – that we'd never even seen when we were in the army doing our compulsory military service.

We were hit by every kind of bomb you can imagine – barrel bombs, cluster bombs, vacuum bombs, phosphorus bombs and chlorine bombs – every different kind of bombardment. In areas where the buildings were harder to destroy, because they were stronger buildings, they would bombard them with big explosive containers that they threw from a helicopter. One of these could destroy a whole building completely.

*

In our crazy world of Aleppo, we became our own saviours. We had to. We found ways of coping. When the street markets were bombed, we lost the fresh fruit and vegetables we loved so much, so people started to grow their own, from seeds, wherever we could – on balconies, on roofs, anywhere we could find a little bit of earth to plant the seeds. We would go to Abu Ward's plant nursery in the Jisr Al-Hajj area near Sukkari. He still sold fruit trees like pears and loquats, along with nut trees like hazelnut and pistachio, and we brought them back to plant in our cat sanctuary and in the children's playground. The ground in both areas was just bare earth, not paving or tarmac, so we could plant things easily. Tomatoes and cucumbers were the best, because they grew the fastest, along with the herbs. It took a lot of effort to keep them going, though, because along with bombing the markets, the bakeries, the hospitals and the schools, our water facilities were also being bombed.

But the animals were no one's priority. Like the people, they too were caught up in all this chaos and were also victims. No one bothered much about them, but I couldn't ignore them. Most of the animals left roaming the streets were cats, sometimes wild, sometimes abandoned pets. Whenever I could, I took them home with me and looked after them. Some were shell-shocked, their sensitive ears traumatized by the loud explosions all around them. Some were injured and there was almost nothing I could do. They needed to be looked after, fed and loved. I stroked them a lot and, in return, they gave me comfort, much needed comfort.

From the last days of May 2016 onwards, things became real hell on earth. That's when it turned into a complete bloodbath, with more and more civilians being killed by the Russian and regime bombing. Three quarters of those killed were civilians, ordinary people who had the bad luck to live in East Aleppo. They were 'guilty by geography', as one foreign journalist described it. Over 5,000 children were killed, just from being in the wrong place at the wrong time. Because for five years we had no proper medicines or vaccinations, infectious diseases like polio, measles and leishmaniosis came back, as if we were plunged into the dark ages. The regime said everyone in East Aleppo was a terrorist – the doctors, the teachers, even people like me who were helping to rescue people caught in their bombing. We heard that the UN Special Envoy for Syria, Staffan de Mistura, put forward a proposal to give East Aleppo autonomy, to break the stalemate. But the regime rejected the plan completely.

Our own government was bombing our markets, bakeries, hospitals, schools and water facilities. There was a method in their madness. They wanted to make it impossible for us to live, to crush us, all for the sake of destroying 'the terrorists'. In June and July 2016, during Ramadan, the Sukhoi jets were even timed deliberately to coincide with *iftaar*, to make sure people couldn't go out to the mosque for the special Ramadan prayers or even prepare food in their kitchens. Everyone had to shelter in their basements waiting for it to be over.

All through this time the outside world was obsessed with the election of Trump as US President and his tweets. What was happening in Syria was pushed to the bottom of the world's agenda and, even though there was lots of film footage of what was happening, the world did not really care. The Russians were closing in on Aleppo. When their aircraft carrier loaded with dozens more Sukhoi jets arrived off the coast in Lattakia, ready to help in the final battle, the regime dropped lots and lots of leaflets warning us to give up. The leaflets said: 'Final Warning – the air strikes will increase. What is coming will be worse. Tomorrow, at

12 o'clock exactly, there will be crushing strikes on this area.' They also sent everyone text messages saying we should leave at once or face death. The government could do this because Syriatel, the main mobile phone company, is owned by Rami Makhlouf, Bashar Al-Assad's cousin, so he controls all the phone data with our numbers.

That was 3 November 2016. Since then, sometimes over thirty barrel bombs and over a hundred artillery shells were dropped on one neighbourhood in a single day. Before that, it counted as a good day if there were only two bombs, and a bad day if there were about ten. Now they were dropping white phosphorus and chlorine bombs, as well as the cluster bombs dropped by the Sukhoi jets and the barrel bombs packed with cheap bits of metal like nails dropped from the helicopters. There were so many dead that the graveyards became full and we had to bury people in parks. But we could only do it at night, and have their funerals in the dark, because it was too dangerous during the day.

We had no weapons to defend ourselves against the Sukhoi jets. We were civilians, and the rebel fighters only had basic weapons, rifles and homemade mortars that couldn't be properly aimed, so they were hopeless at shooting down planes. It was hell for everyone stuck there on the ground.

9: Under Siege

I was passing by the area of Ahmadieh, close to where our cat sanctuary was, when I heard the sound of a dog howling from somewhere high above me. I looked up and saw an Alsatian at the top floor window of a block of flats. He was putting his paws up on the windowsill and crying out.

There was a boy who was living in the building next door, so I asked the child: 'What's the matter with this dog?'

'I'm feeding and taking care of him,' he said.

He explained that the dog's former owner had now left Aleppo with his family. Ahmadieh had been heavily bombed by Russian and Syrian government jets, so the inhabitants had had to flee their homes. Displaced people were leaving chaotically in whatever transport they could find, mostly in *serveeses*, shared minibus taxis, like the ones my uncle and I used to drive. These taxis would never have taken a dog as a passenger, so his owner had left him behind. Rather than abandoning the dog outside on the street, they left him in their home on the fifth floor, the highest floor of the building. This dog wasn't even free inside the flat. He was tied up – they left him there to guard their flat and its possessions from the looting they knew would follow once the regime soldiers entered the area. They imagined they might return one day.

The boy loved dogs and he'd been given the responsibility by the dog's owner of looking after the dog as best he could. He was upset at the thought of the dog dying slowly of starvation all alone, waiting for his owners to return once it was safe, and was vigilant about trying to give the dog some food, whatever scraps he could find. I went up to the top floor with him and made friends with the dog, talking to him and reassuring him in a calm voice and stroking him. He was a very handsome male dog, with black and blond fur. We took him downstairs, played with him, and then I photographed him so that I could introduce him to my Facebook friends in the group. I told them about the child who was taking care of the dog, so they asked me to reward the boy and then to take the dog with me back to the sanctuary.

I had quite a few aggressive stray cats in the sanctuary who couldn't normally live with dogs or with people. Cats and dogs are usually afraid of each other, and I was worried those cats might attack the dog or that he might attack them. So I was hesitant at first and thought that I couldn't bring the dog to the cat sanctuary. But the people in the Facebook group insisted, so I did, on the understanding that

I would have to keep him tied up at first, at least until he could get used to the new place. I said that if he didn't adapt, I would take him to somewhere else, to a friend I knew who liked dogs.

He was a faithful dog, praise be to God. I had to pull him along, because he didn't want to leave his original home. He was loyal and didn't want to stop guarding the apartment for his owners. It was a difficult task taking him back to the sanctuary, but my friends in the Facebook group insisted that he shouldn't be left alone. Eventually I managed to get him back and then I tied him up, as I wanted to protect the cats and to save him from getting lost or from going back to his owner's place. At the sanctuary, at least I could feed him every day and take good care of him.

He was a fine dog and I have lots of photos of him. We decided to call him Hope, because his story was a sign of hope, that we'd managed to save him and that he was now living safely with us. But I refused to let him in amongst the cats. I told my Facebook friends: 'I can't leave him to roam freely in the sanctuary. How can cats and dogs get on?! I'm afraid he'll attack the cats, and bite them. He's not aggressive now, but there's always hate between cats and dogs, unless they have lived together in one house for a long time.'

Hope used to bark at the cats at first, especially when he saw me feeding them as well as him. He didn't dare attack the cats or harm them, though, because he knew that I was taking care of them, as well as taking care of him. I fed him every day and, bit by bit, he got used to them. After two weeks had passed, I was very surprised to notice that Hope had become familiar with the cats and with the sanctuary. He stopped barking at them and scaring them. I would tie him up when the cats were eating, but at night I used to let him off the chain to roam freely.

There were stray dogs in the neighbourhood, and they used to attack the cats at night, so Hope starting defending the sanctuary from them. We often went out when we heard him barking in the evenings, and I would see dogs running away because Hope was attacking them. He would chase the dogs for long distances, and drive them away. The stray dogs were afraid of him. He was very aggressive towards them. He became our guard dog.

These stray dogs were always trying to attack our cats, because they were hungry now that most of the people had left. All they could find to eat, essentially, was cats, but the cats were now safe with me in the sanctuary. So I started to put food out for the stray dogs near the stadium, which was about a kilometre away from us. After I'd finished feeding the cats, I would take any bones and other leftovers and give them to these dogs. The dogs learnt to gather near the stadium and hang around waiting for me to bring the food. But they knew they couldn't come near the sanctuary, because of Hope.

I tried as much as possible to bring the dogs bones

because I couldn't feed them meat – we were in a difficult enough situation ourselves. But then my Facebook friends said to me: 'Why are you bringing them bones? These bones may hurt them and tear their intestines.' I told them: 'These dogs are used to bones, our dogs have iron intestines, and bones don't affect them.' But Europeans don't feed dogs with bones. They asked me to grind the bones for the dogs, so I bought a special machine to grind the bones.

My Facebook friends told me not to tie Hope up, and not to use a chain at all, even during the cats' feeding time. I wasn't convinced it would work, but I started to set him free and watch him. I was amazed to watch as he began to mingle with the cats. He became familiar with them and seemed to like them. The cats would approach him and sit beside him. They even used to eat his food. I have photos showing the cats all around him. They would push him away and eat his food, and he just let them. Can you imagine that? He became a coward, at least with them. There's a Turkish proverb that says: 'Friendship between cats and dogs ends when the butcher's door opens', but, in this case, it didn't happen like that. I think he understood his job now was to protect the cats and to defend them. He was a faithful dog and I learnt a lot from him. Thank God my Facebook friends liked the dog and the people in the neighbourhood liked him as well.

★

For hundreds of years people kept dogs in order to keep cats away, especially if they had birds at home. Lots of people had doves or pigeons or chickens, so they'd keep a dog to stop cats from coming to their house. They often preferred dogs to cats because they believed that dogs were loyal but cats weren't.

In the last period under the siege, dogs began to attack people. This was because stray and abandoned dogs had begun to find dead bodies among the rubble, or in the conflict areas. They found a lot in the Kindi area, in particular. Maybe you heard about it? There were lots of casualties, as the government had deliberately bombed the Kindi Hospital. Nobody could retrieve their bodies, so the stray dogs ate them.

The problem of these dead bodies was one of our biggest fears. We were exposed to wave upon wave of bugs, and people suffered from skin diseases due to the flies and other insects that fed on the dead bodies in the areas where there were so many unburied victims, as they couldn't be reached. There were also lots of dead animals and their bodies couldn't be buried either.

★

Hygiene too was a real problem, both for us and for the cat sanctuary. Our water supply was cut off most of the time, just like the electricity. Hot water was a very rare commodity. In areas that were damaged by shelling, the water pipes were often broken by bombing, which meant that water would simply leak out and be lost. Sometimes you'd see that a bomb crater had filled with water from a leak like this, and local children in the neighbourhood would play in it as if it was a homemade swimming pool. They used it to enjoy themselves, and make the most of it, especially in the hot summer months.

ISIS were in control of Raqqa, Deir Hafir on the Aleppo–Raqqa highway fifty kilometres east of Aleppo, and the Khafsa area on Lake Assad, which had the water pumps for Aleppo. Raqqa was on the Euphrates and controlled the dam upstream at Tabqa. So ISIS cut the water off to the opposition areas, but supplied the regime areas with water. People were saying that the regime was paying them to pump water to regime areas of Aleppo and there were people who said that, because the opposition fighting groups kicked ISIS out of East Aleppo, they had cut off the water to them there. Some said ISIS were taking money from the regime to do this, which is very likely, because the regime always wanted to be in control of things like electricity, power stations and water supplies. The regime wanted to manage these things in whatever way they could, when they couldn't find any other solution.

We had a hard time securing our water supplies. Without water no one can last long, so we had to find our own solution too. This was a big priority, how to secure our water supplies now that the state supply was cut off to us.

We needed a lot of water at the cat sanctuary so that we could clean up. We needed water for washing the cats' bowls and for hosing the area where they ate after every mealtime, to keep it clean and hygienic, to make sure there were no diseases that could spread.

There were wells in other areas further away where we could go to collect water, but we decided we needed to dig wells in our own neighbourhood. I explained this to my Facebook friends in the group. They all supported me. They told me to start working on it and said they would help me. We found ways of digging local wells, to get water for ourselves. It was expensive and needed special equipment and pumps, but we were able to buy the equipment with the money that was being donated to the Ernesto Sanctuary.

Each well cost about 1,000 euros. But of course, when they raised the money, they didn't collect just 1,000 euros. They collected more than that, thanks to the generosity of the group. So what they collected was enough to dig more than one well. We dug one well in the neighbourhood where I lived, and we dug another in the neighbourhood next door. On top of that, we then dug more wells, around five, in several other neighbourhoods. We were worried about running out of water, since it was essential and so precious.

The electricity was also cut off totally. If we didn't have diesel, we couldn't get the generators working to generate our own electricity, so that meant we couldn't get the water out of the wells, because we needed electric pumps to get the water up. We were very careful with how we used the wells. We rationed the amount of pumping time we needed to get enough water out, and how much diesel we needed to use for that, because we wanted to be on the safe side in the future. We thought that if we reached a critical point where we were in danger of running out of water, we should warn people. We needed to be aware of our water consumption.

There was a young man with us who was very good at maths and arithmetic and he was able to calculate the consumption of water accurately and to work out how much should be distributed to each family, as well as to the street storage tanks. Each day we had to fill the water storage tanks in the neighbourhood with 2,000 litres of water, enough to provide the whole neighbourhood. We used to pump the water up out of the wells, and so that it was safe to drink, we used to add chlorine to sterilize the water. Some organizations used to give us chlorine tablets. We added one tablet for every 100 litres of water. So we added about twenty tablets to each tank of water, which then sterilized it completely, and kept it free of germs and microbes for a long time. We were afraid it might contain germs or algae. But if you sterilize water you can save it for a year, and it won't change or go bad.

We advised people in our neighbourhood to take their drinking water from these tanks in the street, and the water which we got straight out of the wells, the untreated water, we pumped direct into their houses to be used for washing clothes and for bathing. We agreed on a man to be in charge of our water system, and for each well there was a man whose responsibility it was to fill the tank beside it. Children would come to drink directly from the tap on the tank, or to fill their bottles.

Food was, of course, the other big problem during the siege in Aleppo. We had to be very organized, just like we were with the water. At the beginning of the crisis, before Aleppo was fully besieged, the bombardment first intensified on the Castello Road, the only entrance to the eastern part of the city. The shelling continued for more than two months, so the food began to decrease. Supplies started to drop and prices shot up. Some food could still be brought into the city, but it started to get rarer and rarer.

It was at this point that my friends in the Facebook group asked me to leave Aleppo and to take the cats with me. I told them that I couldn't. I had to stay with the people, with my neighbours. I couldn't just take the cats and run away, but I did agree to evacuate individual cats if an opportunity arose. If friends around me were leaving, I asked if they were able to take a cat with them.

When I made the decision to stay, my friends in the Facebook group told me that I must at least make a food store. We knew that the siege was coming, and that the roads in and out of Aleppo could soon be blocked. I agreed with them that it was a good idea, because everyone would benefit from this, people as well as the animals. We didn't know how long the siege would last. It could be months or years. I received a big fund for this from donations to the Facebook group – it amounted to 20,000 euros.

Using this money, I stored enough food to feed 2,000 people for a year and half. I bought food that would keep and not go off: five tonnes of rice, three tonnes of bulgur wheat, three tonnes of oil and ghee, hundreds of tins of food, packets of soup and lentils. I put it all in a store. We could only realistically help our own neighbourhood, not all of Aleppo, of course, so we decided to help those 2,000 people who lived in the immediate area around the cat sanctuary. There were around 130 families or more. I stored food for these 2,000 individuals as well as for the animals.

Storing the food reminded me of something one of my Facebook friends had told me about the ancient Egyptians, about how cats were given a special reverence back then because they protected their most valuable thing – their granaries – from mice and rats. How, for them, a cat's life was as important as a human's life. If someone killed a cat, they would even be executed or lynched by a mob. Rich owners would groom their cats, bathe them and anoint them with oil as if they were royalty, and always feed them excellent food. So, even if there was a famine, they still gave food to the cats, to make sure that the cats could carry on protecting the precious grain harvest on which they all depended. It's funny, but it makes me think of what we had to do during the siege of Aleppo, which was like a famine, to be honest. We had to store all our rice and bulgur wheat on the first floor of buildings, not on the ground floor. If we'd put it on the ground floor, it would've been eaten by the mice and the rats. We had all the cats safely in the sanctuary, after all, so they weren't out killing these vermin. It makes me laugh that, like the ancient Egyptians, our most precious treasure was our grain. My Facebook friends told me that there's an ancient Egyptian book written on papyrus, which says that, if a man sees himself in a dream looking at a big cat, it's a good omen, because it means that a big harvest will come to him. I'm still waiting to have a dream like this.

★

I bought a large amount of the food at a high price, because many people had already begun to store food, so prices had increased. They were high because it was so very difficult to get foodstuff through the Castello Road. The regime and the Kurds were already targeting it, so it was very dangerous for trucks and cars to enter the city with provisions. This made prices very high.

Once I was almost lucky enough to get a car full of food-stuffs. The driver had left it and run away, because a shell had hit the car and smashed the windscreen. We had a kind of surveillance set up in the area to check on the road, so that we could see if a vehicle had been hit by shelling and if someone inside might be injured. So, when the surveillance people saw that the vehicle had been hit and wasn't moving, they called by radio for an ambulance. I went immediately with my ambulance car, because I knew the area very well. I drove up to the stopped vehicle, looking for the driver or for any passengers who might need help. I couldn't see the driver or anyone inside, but the keys were still inside the vehicle, so I knocked a hole in the windscreen so that I could see out, then I drove it back into Aleppo. It was carrying lots of bags of potatoes, among other things.

A journalist friend was with me at the time, and I told him that I wanted to take this car into Aleppo, because of all the foodstuffs and potatoes it was carrying, even if it meant I had to leave my own car there. So I left my own ambulance, since there were no victims, and I drove the vehicle with the potatoes to the Jandool Roundabout. My friend the journalist followed me, driving my ambulance.

At the Jandool Roundabout, there were men who waited to help any injured people. They were volunteers. They told me that the driver of the vehicle had reached the Ba'edin Roundabout, which is the next roundabout along. They called there to say that the vehicle with the potatoes whose driver had abandoned it was now safely at the Jandool Roundabout. So the driver came back and collected his vehicle and drove it on into Aleppo.

Thanks to a mixture of what I was able to buy with the donations from abroad, and any foodstuffs we were able to save or rescue, I succeeded in storing a huge amount of food. So I stayed on in Aleppo, and when the bombardment intensified on the Castello Road, I was in that area a lot in my rescue and ambulance work, transferring victims to the hospitals. A lot of the families were fleeing because of the heavy regime bombing and, more often than not, they were getting caught on the Castello Road. It became incredibly dangerous to travel along this route, but it was the only way in or out of the city for people like us who lived in East Aleppo. My wife and children had been so lucky to get out before the siege.

The regime was also bombing the road from Shaikh Youssef and several other areas, like Mallah. They were hitting the roads so that it was difficult for people to leave. There were so many victims, including women and children. And there were a lot of people whose clothes caught fire from all the bombs and the explosions. They were being burnt alive even though we would do our best to put out the flames.

The army gradually closed in on the city of Aleppo until the day we carried that last victim from the Castello Road – the man with the Eid gifts. After that, there was no way in or out.

Now that we were trapped inside the city, we had to be even more careful with the resources we had. We started to use the stored food very carefully, especially the meat. But even from the beginning of the siege, there was no chicken meat. This was the meat I normally used to feed the cats, so because we couldn't get chicken meat anymore, I cooked rice and mixed it with tinned luncheon meat. A tin of meat was so expensive. Even a very small tin of meat, when I could find it, cost 6 Euros, which is nearly US$7. I mixed them together in order to give the rice, which bulked things out, a meaty taste, to at least attempt to make the cats feel that it was real meat. Some of the cats ate it, but many didn't. It was difficult. I tried it for three days with them, until, in the end, they got used to eating it. They had to eat it, even though it was more rice than meat. It was better than nothing.

After three days they all began to eat it normally and even finished their plates. It was the first time they'd ever eaten rice. They were used to eating chicken meat, but in the end they adapted to the change in diet. Sometimes I cooked rice flavoured with chicken soup and tomato paste for them as a change. That was for the first month and a half, the first forty-five days of the siege.

After two months, I started to cook the same food for people and for cats, in order to save the tinned luncheon meat and the tinned chicken meat that we had, so I cooked the rice flavoured with chicken soup and tomato paste more and more. I cooked it and distributed it to the families in our neighbourhood, to the 2,000 people, and I left some over for cats. I used to mix the soup either with rice or with bulgur wheat. The cats, it turned out, loved it. It was as if the cats understood that we were under siege and that no meat was left, so they had to learn to eat people's food. They'd been used to eating meat for a year and a half prior to that in the cat sanctuary, but within a few days they learnt to eat rice and bulgur wheat with soups, as well as the leftover food from the communal kitchen that we'd set up during the siege.

Of course they got ill, of course they did. When it started to show and be obvious that they were not well, a friend of mine who was a vet told me that they were all going to die one by one. He told me that, if cats don't eat fresh meat for more than a month, they begin to lose their muscles. 'They need protein,' he said. 'Cats have 500 muscles, so they need a lot of protein and meat.' I told him that we had meat, that we had butchers who sold lamb and beef, but that for Muslims it was forbidden – *haraam*, as we call it in Arabic – to feed lamb and beef meat to animals, if people couldn't afford to buy the meat themselves.

However, we decided I had to give them fresh meat once a week, to try to keep them alive and healthy. The only way I could do this, and comply with our Islamic rule about people needing to have meat before cats, was for me to buy fresh meat from the butcher for cooking, and then to cook for people and cats together. That way, the cats could eat meat. So I started to do that, to feed the cats meat once or twice a week. I bought thirty-five kilogrammes of meat every day, to feed the neighbourhood. I asked the butcher to bring me the same amount every day, so that I could cook for people and also feed the cats. We continued like that for five months. One kilogramme of meat cost 7,000 Syrian pounds, about 15 euros. It was very expensive.

Sometimes I wondered what the cats thought about all this, what they thought about their lifestyle and how it changed during the war. I wondered if some of them were with the opposition and some were with the regime. In the end I decided that they were probably against all of us, against all mankind. They had all suffered, thanks to us humans. Many cats that had once been nice became aggressive, because of the bombing and because of their fear. When a cat heard the sound of a plane or a shell or even gunfire, it would often think that the nearest person was responsible for that; they thought that he must be the person who is causing this somehow. Some cats stopped coming to me for this reason. There were some who liked to be stroked by me, but many cats kept their distance and wouldn't let me play with them anymore. It became difficult to touch them and to get close to them. Of course the cats couldn't tell the difference between occasional opposition mortars and constant regime bombing. The cats had no idea – it was all the same to them. So the first person they saw was the person they thought was responsible for the bombing and the explosions. I often looked at them and wondered if they thought it was somehow my fault, what was happening all around them.

★

In November 2016, the day we had feared came: the Aleppo cat sanctuary was bombed. I was there when it happened, hiding as the Russian and Syrian fighter jets approached. The whole area was bombed, with missiles, artillery and air strikes. I was watching from the window, and saw how the missiles landed. They hit the courtyard of the sanctuary and I could hear Hope howling. I thought he was howling from fear. He was tied up and I hoped I might be able to set him free, but I was afraid to go outside while we were under attack. He was in the kennel that I'd made for him. Then I saw that a shell had hit his kennel.

As suddenly as the bombardment began, it was over. Thank God, I was still alive. But my sanctuary was lost. Afterwards, we went outside to see the damage. There was shrapnel everywhere, and many cats were dead. Hope was lying on the ground. I hate to remember this. He was very badly injured in his chest and his paws were crushed. The bones of his legs were smashed and he needed surgery. He needed to have his leg amputated, but it was impossible even to treat people at this time, so how could it be possible to treat a dog? Even if we took him to the hospital, the doctor wouldn't have helped him.

He was suffering and howling with pain. We had to

choose, either to let him be tortured by his wounds or end his life to save him from suffering. I remembered hearing from my grandparents that if we can help an animal by helping it to recover, we must help it, but that if we can't help it, we must show mercy and give it a merciful death. We must kill it so it doesn't suffer. That is what our religion, Islam, teaches us. There was no cure for Hope. We couldn't treat him. I couldn't bear to hear his howling. It was too painful for me. So I asked my friend to end his life. I hid while he did it, because I couldn't watch.

We also ended the lives of many cats, because it was impossible to save them. We gave them the shot of mercy, firing a bullet into their brain. I know it is the same think-ing with horses, when their legs are broken. People kill them so that they don't suffer more than necessary; the bullet is more merciful than letting the creature suffer, because we can't help. So we had to kill any animal that was dying. If their injury was minor, we tried to treat them ourselves as best we could, but we couldn't give them sur-gery if their injuries were in their bodies or in their stomachs, or if their bones were smashed. So we had to kill them.

Twelve cats were killed in front of me from shrapnel wounds during the bombing. The injured cats ran away if they were able to move. I could tell this, because, after-wards, when we were looking for the cats, I saw trails of blood on the ground. After the bombardment had moved away to a different area, we went out to look for the cats. I was feeling very upset and confused because of Hope, and the destruction around me. We tried to take any cats we could find away to another place, away from the sanctuary. We prepared a special room as best we could on the ground floor of a neighbouring building, to hide them away from danger.

Many, many cats were killed, I think more than forty. When the shelling stopped, I put food out, trying to gather them again and to collect them. To stop them running away, I picked them up while they were eating, then took them to the new place we'd prepared nearby. I was surprised to see that just forty to fifty cats came to eat. On that first day of shelling, I lost more than a hundred cats, including the injured ones, the dead ones and the ones that ran away and which I never saw again.

Our ordeal wasn't over, because the cats that survived the shelling were then affected by a gas bombing the next day. The regime planes dropped chlorine bombs on us. The cats didn't know how to flee to the upper floors to escape the poison gas, so they stayed on the lower floors and were poisoned. I didn't know where they were, because they were hiding in the nearby buildings. After the chlorine bombing, only about thirty of the cats were left. The next day we took them to another place, away from that area.

It affected us deeply. We were traumatized by the bombing of the sanctuary and from losing Hope and so many cats because of the shrapnel and the chlorine gas. It seemed that his name, Hope, had been the wrong choice. With his death, our hope died too.

10: Escape

It became impossible to stay in Hanano after those final fifteen days of continuous bombardment. I had to move, along with many other desperate people, to a different area. The whole Hanano Housing District emptied out and was abandoned, leaving just the shells of the destroyed buildings, our cat sanctuary among them.

After that I had to move three more times, to different houses, within a brief period, because the shelling in the whole wider neighbourhood of East Aleppo was so intense. The regime and the Russians were bombing us day and night. First I moved to an area called Karm Al-Jabal, close to Al-Sha'ar, where I lived for just two weeks. Then I had to move again when clashes came to the area, so I moved to the area of Ansari, where I stayed for the final month. It was near Sukkari Square, between Saif Al-Dawla, Salaheddin and Sukkari, in an area called Al-Ansari Al-Sharqi. Sukkari is on the left and Tell Al-Zarazeer is on the right, near the Hajj bridge towards Sukkari. This was the last area still in the hands of the opposition groups, the area where people were forced to gather because everywhere else had been bombed. But even that final brief home of mine in Ansari was destroyed in the end. The whole building was bombed by Russian fighter jets.

But throughout it all I still had my cats with me, including Ernesto, Sukhoi 25 and Sukhoi 26. I had about sixteen cats, in all: the ones who survived the bombing of the sanctuary and the chlorine gas attack. The rest were kept safe by other people who'd also been displaced from Hanano. We took them with us after we had to leave the destroyed neighbourhood and the sanctuary.

I put the cats into an empty shop that still had a working metal shutter. I made sure they were safe and I kept the shutter locked, because I was afraid to let them out in case they got injured in the bombing or got lost. We were a long way from Hanano by this point, so this was a completely new area for them, which they didn't know at all. It would have been very confusing for them to be let out, and I knew I probably wouldn't find them again. So I fed them inside this empty shop. The families who had the other cats were all living close by. I used to go and see them and take them food. I'd been helping these families anyway, for a long time before this, so they helped me in return by sheltering the cats I couldn't take with me.

Two of them were friends who used to help me at Ernesto's Sanctuary. If I was away rescuing people, or was late back, they used to feed the cats for me. Often I was late because it was so difficult to drive back, as I kept having to wait and hide because there were so many fighter jets. As soon as one left another would come along. There was non-stop bombardment from aircraft, artillery and missiles all through November and December 2016. I am sure you heard about it on your news channels.

Nothing that had gone before prepared us for this bombardment of Aleppo. It was even more horrific than what happened later in the Ghouta, in February and March 2018. When we passed through the streets on our way to rescue people, buildings would collapse around us. It was like something from an action movie. Rocks and stones kept falling in front of us or hitting the car. Our wind-screens even smashed from the loudness of the shelling. We suffered far beyond what can possibly be imagined. For a period of about twenty days we could hardly sleep, even for ten minutes. Fifteen minutes or one hour would have seemed like a luxury, but we couldn't even snatch a bare ten minutes' rest. Those last days of the siege in Aleppo at the end of 2016 were very, very hard.

*

When areas like Al-Shaar, the road to Al-Bab and Bab An-Nayrab – all of which were targeted after Hanano – were first bombed, there were lots of people crowded together in the streets trying to flee, so there were lots of injuries. There was also an area in the Old City, near Jowb

Al-Quba and close to Bab Al-Hadeed, where there's a wide street. People were there in large numbers, flowing along like a river, trying to escape. They were hit by missiles there in the street. Many were killed. The families were fleeing from place to place on foot. There were no cars. Many, many people died and were injured in the chaos, most of them children. Just imagine these missiles landing in the middle of 300 or more people. All of them were hurt, if not worse.

When we went there to try to help them, the missiles were still falling from above. Driving along in the ambulance, we hid more than four times to avoid the shelling from aircraft and the artillery guns. The aircraft were able to monitor our movements much better than the artillery guns, so the planes bombed us first and then the machine guns would follow up and carry on firing shells on the same area. They recognized the target by the smoke and dust that billowed up out of the place the aircraft had just bombed. Buildings crowded with people were bombed. The aircraft and the machine guns synchronized their actions, working side by side, determined to make sure that no injured person could be rescued.

We used to go to these areas to help people, but there were places that were impossible to reach by car, because the roads were blocked by fallen debris and destroyed buildings. So sometimes we had to go on foot to reach some of those places where there were injured people.

Escape

It was a desperate and miserable situation. We took as many injured people as we could to the hospital, but there were still so many other people left trapped under the rubble. We could hear them begging for help. Many of them were children. We witnessed and lived through so many gruesome and harrowing incidents, and often had to decide whether to take the people we'd rescued straight to the hospital to get treatment to stop them dying, or whether to stay and try to rescue more people who were still calling out for help from underneath the rubble. There was a shortage of ambulances too. The area was bombed continuously for 24 hours without break, so wherever we moved there would be ever more shells falling around us all the time. It was beyond what anyone should have to bear.

The most painful and upsetting cases were when we could hear that there were children still trapped under the rubble, but we couldn't get to them, as sometimes it needed heavy machinery and we weren't equipped. We could hear them shouting for help and screaming. Many people were left trapped under the rubble while still alive.

In the Lose Dam area, I rescued four injured people with my car, but I could hear that there were still children left under the rubble crying. There was nothing I could do for them, I swear by God. It would have needed a forklift or a crane to remove the concrete roof that was trapping them. Twenty people working together wouldn't have been able to remove it, even if we hadn't had the non-stop shelling overhead. It was excruciating, having to leave people under the rubble to die.

In the makeshift hospitals, which were mainly underground for protection from attack, we put people down in the corridors, on chairs and in every space we could find. The hospitals were full of victims. There were no medicines and not enough doctors. People bled to death, because no one could treat them in time. The situation was so bad that we ended up assuming that any injured person was certain to die. In some ways, it was better for those who died instantly. Those who survived, but were injured, would suffer terribly and then die anyway, especially if they were bleeding heavily. When we ran in and out of the hospitals with our wounded victims, it began to feel as if we were walking on red soil. You know what red earth looks like when it gets mixed with water? That was what the blood looked like on the floor of the hospital. The layer of blood was so deep it was the width of two fingers. Our shoes became completely clogged with it. These were the toughest days, at what turned out to be the very end of the siege. It was tragic and traumatic what we went through in rescuing these people. We felt sure we were going to die too. We prayed to God to let us be killed in the bombing, rather than injured. We wished for death, not injury. Death was preferable in those terrible times.

When the final truce between the regime and the opposition came in December 2016, everything was so confusing.

The regime said they were sending buses to transfer us out to Idlib, the next-door province that was still under opposition control. All the fighters and armed groups forced out from places that had surrendered, like Homs and Wadi Barada, near Damascus, had been sent there as a kind of chaotic and lawless dumping ground, to be dealt with later. I think they hoped that, by confining everyone there, they'd all end up killing each other and save them the trouble. The green government buses that they were proposing to use to transport us were already well known from the other 'starve and surrender' sieges the regime had conducted, before Aleppo. The buses were supposed to be coming on 14 December, but there were repeated delays because the negotiations kept breaking down. We were told it was pro-regime Iran and their Shi'ite militias who were behind the problems.

The streets were full of people, waiting, confused, desperate, not knowing their future, and we had to keep the cats in cages all the time, to stop them running away in panic. They had to be fed in the cages too, so their behaviour changed a lot. We didn't have enough proper cages, so some had to be in plastic crates that were used for vegetables. In the chaos and confusion, three escaped and it was impossible to catch them in the crowds. It was 15 December 2016, so it had been almost exactly a month since the sanctuary had been bombed. They, like us, had been through so much, and they were panicky and very frightened.

Those final stages of the evacuation were very hard. There were 3,000 people who were critically injured and needed to be transferred out by ambulance. Can you imagine that? We were told they had to be transferred out within 48 hours maximum, and the Syrian Red Crescent was in charge of making this happen. But the Red Crescent ambulances could only carry one wounded person at a time, because that's how they're designed. Though sometimes they could also take one additional wounded person, if they could sit, because they have one chair as well. But our ambulances had originally been minivans, so they were just empty spaces in the back and could easily take four injured people lying down in a row. So we said to the Red Crescent people: 'You're just taking one person and it'll take you four or five hours to reach the place in the western countryside where the injured people are gathered before they're transferred to Turkey. Why don't you let us move them too with our ambulances? It's a humanitarian case.'

But the Red Crescent is under regime control and cannot break with the guidelines. They said: 'Our orders say we must just carry one person at a time.' So then we spoke to their sister organisation, the Red Cross, who were also there, and they were more reasonable and agreed: 'You can transfer all the wounded people in your ambulances. Use all your ambulances.'

So I left with the second group and we made the Red Crescent ambulances drive in front, so that we could drive out of the city in convoy with them. All four of our ambulances from the cat sanctuary drove out together, each one with four injured people in the back, together with their families. Each injured person had a family, of course, so we took their wives and children with them. Imagine how crowded our ambulances were, with the four injured people and their families. The injured people were begging us to take their families with them, because they didn't want their families to go on the green buses and be separated from them. Each wounded person was to be taken straight to the border to enter Turkey, and if their family was with them, they could enter too. If they were alone, their family would never be allowed to join them later in Turkey, and it was forbidden for them to cross legally. The border was closed except for urgent medical cases.

At first the Red Crescent people refused to take the families in their ambulances with their one injured person, but in the end we persuaded them. We argued with them: 'Why don't you take his family with him? Why should his wife and children be left alone? Who will take care of his wife and children?' There was a lot of confusion throughout this process of transferring the injured people out of Aleppo.

The Russians were there, checking all the ambulances, and they asked me: 'How many people are there in your car? How many injured?' I told the Russian: 'I have nine people inside the ambulance with me. And a cat.' The Russian laughed when he saw Ernesto. I had left almost everything behind in Aleppo, but kept my favourite T-shirt folded up on the dashboard for Ernesto to sleep on. It was comforting, because it had my smell, so he happily curled up on that spot for the entire journey. The Russian thought it was so funny to see a cat with me that he didn't notice I actually had six in the ambulance.

As for the remaining cats, while we were still in Aleppo waiting to be evacuated, I'd put them in plastic vegetable crates with holes in and given them to the other families from our neighbourhood. I gave each family two cats. These people weren't injured, so they had to wait to travel out on the green government buses and they had to wait for the ambulances, including the four ambulances from our cat sanctuary, to leave first with the injured. Accompanied by the Red Crescent ambulances, we drove out of the city in convoy towards the western countryside, but the Red Crescent ambulances didn't go any further than the assigned gathering point, while we drove straight to the Turkish border and dropped the injured people and their families there.

After turning back from the Turkish border, we didn't return to Aleppo but instead headed to the gathering point in the western countryside, where the ambulances with the other injured people were waiting. Unlike us, the Red Crescent ambulances were just shuttling them from Aleppo to this point, and then they'd leave them there, so we used our ambulances to transfer them onwards to the Turkish border. Some of the injured were brought out of Aleppo using private cars, but they were also just left at this gathering point. It took us twelve days to evacuate all the injured people from the gathering point and take them to the Turkish border. I have photos from that time which show how we were helping the wounded people and their children, distributing food to them, especially kids' food, like sweets, which they hadn't had for so long under the siege. We felt happy that these people from Aleppo, some of whom knew us, had been saved from bombing and from hunger, and although it was an exhausting time and very hard work, it gave us some satisfaction to know that these people were now safe.

During those twelve days I also made arrangements to settle the cats. Some of the families who'd helped carry them out went off to different places in the northern part of the Aleppo countryside, where they had relations, and they took the cats they had with them. Wherever possible it was best for the cats to stay with a family. Some families, however, gave me the cats back. Among the ones that stayed with me were Ernesto, Sukhoi 25 and Sukhoi 26.

★

I had been running on adrenaline for so long that everything that had happened only began to sink in once my friends, cats and I were all safe. I was so confused and upset by the trauma of all I had been through and I had no idea what the future held for me. My dream, I felt, was over.

Alessandra and my friends from the Facebook group called me and told me to meet them in Turkey. They knew I was completely depressed and devastated and they wanted to try to help me and support me at this critical time, to ease my grief after the loss of the sanctuary and my home. I also hadn't seen my family for a long time, at least a year and a half, so I wanted to go to Istanbul to see my children.

This journey to Turkey was right at the end of 2016, after the fall of Aleppo. It took me four days to cross the border, but eventually I was able to get across, thanks to the help of some NGOs who knew my work. They gave me a document to say I was a worker from Turkey who'd been in Syria for a trip and was now returning to Turkey. It wasn't possible for me to enter legally – only injured people were allowed to enter legally, so we had to use this trick.

When I finally crossed into Turkey at Kilis, my friends, including Alessandra, were waiting for me at the border. They were very happy to see me and they tried hard to cheer me up and to give me emotional support. They felt so sorry about what had happened. Some of them advised me to leave Syria for good and to go to Europe. 'It's hard now to stay in Syria,' they told me. 'We'll help you to go to any European country where you can still practise your hobby of looking after cats.'

After my wife left me and took our children, I had often

thought about what my life would have been like if I had joined them in Turkey. My marriage had not survived the war and I missed my children terribly. If I had gone with them that day, life would have been easier. I would not have experienced many of the gruelling things I went through in Aleppo. I know too that many Syrian refugees are happier in their new lives in Europe, away from conflict and pain. But I don't believe I can be one of those people. Aleppo is my home. Syrians are my people. Helping those in need is my life's work.

So, I told my friends: 'I have to go back.' I felt very strongly that there were people in Syria who still needed my help, as well as animals. I couldn't just abandon them.

They understood that I was serious, so after discussing it carefully, we agreed I would go back and establish a new sanctuary and perhaps even work much harder and be even more ambitious than before, because now I would be close to the Turkish border, where I could get food easily and everything else we needed. While we were in Aleppo under the siege, it was always very difficult to get enough food for the cats, which limited what I could do.

I promised them I would set out to find a new place where I could create a new sanctuary for the surviving cats I'd managed to bring out from the old destroyed sanctuary in Aleppo. We even decided to try and build it bigger and better than before and they reassured me they would collect funds to help me buy a new vehicle, as that way I could even continue with any ambulance and rescue work that might be needed at the new site, since it would obviously have to be located in an area under opposition control. To go to a regime-controlled area would be impossible because they'd consider me a terrorist for remaining in Aleppo; I'd be arrested and almost certainly imprisoned. Everyone in the group promised to support me. It was a big comfort, knowing we had a plan for the future.

But first I needed a break from the trauma of the final eviction from Aleppo, some time to recover from the tensions and extreme stresses of those final months under siege, when I'd witnessed so many terrible things. We arrived in Istanbul during the last days of 2016, and my friends suggested it would be nice to spend New Year's Eve together. I was exhausted by then and keen to spend as much time as possible resting and relaxing with my family and children, but I agreed to join their celebrations.

On the night itself we went to a very crowded place on the Bosphorus Bridge where there are lots of restaurants and nightclubs. We were standing on the bridge taking photos when suddenly I heard shooting. I shouted to my friends: 'Quick! We must run away to be safe!' but they assured me it was just fireworks and nothing to worry about. I insisted: 'I know the sound of shooting very well and I know the sound of fireworks very well. Believe me, we need to run away!'

Moments later we saw people crawling out of the restaurant next door to ours and they were bleeding. It was a terrorist attack. My friends hadn't believed me until they saw the blood on the ground and the people lying there. We left the area as fast as we could, but we had to walk until about 4 a.m. before we could find a taxi to get us home. The streets were full of security forces and ambulances, but no normal cars at all. All private cars had been forbidden from leaving or entering the area. Even our taxi driver had just run away and abandoned his car.

It was a crazy time for Istanbul, but for me it was almost normal. I even joked to my friends: 'It's just like Aleppo when an area was bombed – only with fire engines and ambulances on the streets! The only difference is that here the lights are on, but in Aleppo it was always dark and cars never put their lights on!'

My friends were shaken by their experience of this terrorist attack. One friend said: 'It's as if God wanted to make us feel for just one night what you had to suffer all these years.' The people killed in that Istanbul terrorist incident were mainly Arabs from Jordan and Saudi Arabia. The rest were locals and other foreigners, mainly tourists. The attack was later claimed by ISIS, and turned out to have been carried out by a man dressed up in a Santa Claus costume.

*

My friends left a week later and I stayed on with my children for another three weeks. I finally started to relax and allowed myself to enjoy spending lots of time with them. It was a beautiful few weeks.

Istanbul, as you may know, is full of cats and while I was there I met a special one. I was walking with my brother-in-law, my wife's brother, on the way back to my children's house, when I saw this cat and called for him to come to me. But my brother-in-law laughed and said: 'He's a Turkish cat. You need to talk to him in Turkish.' So he taught me how to say 'Come' in Turkish and then the cat came to me. I picked him up and carried him with me for about ten metres, but then I realized he was a very clean cat, completely blond, so I thought he must be someone's pet. In Turkey people look after cats, and I didn't want to make him leave his home area, so I left him and walked away.

About an hour later, we arrived home and my brother-in-law turned around and set off to work. But then he came straight back and said: 'Alaa, guess who's outside? The cat we saw, the pretty blond one.' I didn't believe it at first, because we had left him a long way away, and so I assumed he must have mistaken the cat, but he said: 'I think the cat followed you somehow and he's now waiting outside the house.' I opened the door and the cat walked straight inside! He was a wonderful cat; good natured and calm and I was very happy with him. My children loved him too and we played with him together.

It was such a surprise. How had that cat crossed such a long distance to come to me? Did he really like me that much? When I'd first seen him, I'd only held him for a minute before putting him down. I thought of taking him back to where I'd first seen him, but my brother-in-law had seen the cat before and thought he must be a stray. He said: 'If he were somebody's cat, he wouldn't follow you.'

So we decided to put food for him outside the house, just in case, but he always wanted to come inside. By that point I was convinced he didn't belong to anyone, so I took care of him during my stay in Istanbul. I decided to take him back to Syria with me, as a reminder of the special time I'd spent with my children. I felt I needed him. We called him Firas, after a friend.

★

When my time in Turkey was over, I began my long journey home again. I was going to smuggle myself back into Syria. With a cat.

I put Firas in a cat cage, and booked a special seat next to me on the bus from Istanbul. When we finally arrived at the Syrian border, it was pouring with rain and difficult to see. I tried to smuggle myself across on foot, carrying the cat cage and my bag. Everything got covered with mud, including me and Firas.

But the Turkish border police caught us. I'd heard from lots of people that these border guards are very tough on people they catch. They dragged us off into their border hut. It seemed weird to them that a Syrian man wanted to cross back *into* Syria, especially with a cat. I think it was the first time they'd seen anything like it. They couldn't believe how I could help a cat at a time like this when it should have been me, as a Syrian, who needed help. Of course, they didn't know that this cat was Turkish. They thought I'd taken it out of Syria with me, then back again.

I expected the worst. Then I remembered that I had some European magazines with pictures of me and my work. Alessandra had given them to me in Istanbul. I took them out of my bag and showed the guards the articles with photos of me, my ambulance and my cats. We couldn't really understand each other, except with sign language, but the officer in charge knew a handful of words in Arabic. 'This is you?' he said, pointing to the pictures. 'Yes, it's me,' I assured him. When he realized it was true, he called to the border guards to give me my luggage back and said to me: 'Syria no, Syria *Daesh*, don't go to Syria.' They wanted me to stay in Turkey. It was funny the way one minute they were treating me roughly, the next minute they were worried about me. When they understood I really wanted to go back, they put my luggage in their car and gave me time to clean myself and wash all the mud off. They even played with Firas and brought their dog to say hello. Firas wasn't very friendly back; he's a strong cat and wanted to defend himself.

Before letting me go, the officer told me: 'You can't continue into Syria legally without an official paper to say you left Turkey legally.' It was very late by then, so I went to a hotel, but the hotel manager didn't allow pets. I changed hotel and the new hotel let me keep Firas with me on condition I kept him in the cage, but when I got to my room I let Firas out and gave him food and water. Then he slept beside me.

The next day I arranged for papers to make it look as if I'd exited Syria legally and entered Turkey legally, so that I could then go back in again legally. I had papers with me translated into Turkish saying I was on a visit to Turkey, that I'd been under siege in Aleppo and that I'd wanted to see my children in Istanbul. Turks like people from Aleppo, so I never had any trouble travelling inside Turkey. My difficulties began only once I wanted to re-enter Syria. But I'll never forget that Turkish border officer, who treated me respectfully because of my humanitarian work inside Syria.

★

Once I was over the border, I contacted my friends in the Facebook group and told them I'd arrived inside Syria safely with Firas. They already knew the full story about him, how I'd found him and how he'd followed me, because I'd told them all about it when I was in Turkey. They were glad to hear that I'd carried Firas from the streets of Istanbul to Syria, and laughed a lot about the absurdity of the situation – that I was smuggling him back into Syria.

Firas didn't seem to mind, though. He was just happy to

be off the streets and with me. He never left me, and followed me everywhere. At the beginning it was hard to make him understand that sometimes I had to go out to do some work but that I would always return. He wanted to follow me wherever I went. He's my best companion. He reminds me of my own children in Istanbul and gives me strength.

11: A Sanctuary for Everyone

Ernesto's Paradise is the name of our new sanctuary. It is in an area close to Al-Dana near the Turkish border crossing of Bab Al-Hawa, about forty-five kilometres from Aleppo. Lots of people from Aleppo used to travel to this area for their summer holidays, as I did as a child with my family, because it was cooler outside the city. There are attractive villas and gardens there, and countryside all around full of farms with olive and pistachio trees. It's a very pretty area, such a contrast from our first simple sanctuary in Aleppo, which was just a patch of earth that we tried to make attractive by planting trees and flowers.

The first funds I received towards the new sanctuary were from an NGO, a sum of US$10,000. With that money I bought first the land and then the villa where we set up the sanctuary in May 2017. The land is like a kind of farm beside the villa.

Many of my friends from the Facebook group supported me too. When we started the new sanctuary, we realized we'd need lots of extra help with the fund-raising. Our plans were very ambitious, but a special cat came to us at exactly the right moment. We found him when he was still very young. He was a stray and his colouring is very distinctive. He looks like a tiger, with a mix of black and gold stripes. One of my friends in the group told me you get this kind of cat in Europe, so we thought he must be of European origin. You rarely see other cats like him. We called him Maxi.

Maxi attracted the attention of many of the members of the Facebook group – we have thousands of members and Twitter followers from all over the world now. They really like how he moves his mouth: when he meows, he opens his mouth completely, so it looks enormous and very wide. It almost seems like he's mocking us when he does it and so my friends in the Facebook group enjoy making up stories about him.

His meow is also very loud, and so we joke that he's always shouting. We've given him the title of 'King of the Cats', because his behaviour is very bossy. We even do little performances with him, dressing him up in a red royal gown and a golden crown, as befits his nickname. He became our 'marketing cat', and we decided Maxi was the perfect 'frontman' for our fundraising campaigns.

One funny scenario we staged with Maxi was to make him look like a barber, as if he owned a hair salon for cats. Then we'd post messages from him offering to do special hairstyles for donors. Another time we made him look like a juice seller, calling him the 'King of Juices', and making it look like he was offering juice or lemonade to the other cats. We also started the idea of donors adopting a cat or a kitten they liked, so lots of people in the group adopted cats in the sanctuary, and then Maxi the King asks them if they'd like to buy some juice for their adopted cats. We take pictures of him like this, dressed in his royal robes and crown, opening up the juice bar. Then we put up another sign in the photo saying 'This is Ernesto's Paradise', with a label above the juice stand saying 'Wine Bar'. So Maxi the King entertains people round the world and at the same time raises funds for the sanctuary. He's our spokesperson. One of the photos even shows him with lots of microphones arranged in front of him, as if he's giving a speech or making a statement. It looks like he's a leader or a president.

We pretend that I work for Maxi, who gives me my orders. We even made new T-shirts in yellow as a kind of uniform for everyone at the sanctuary. My T-shirt says 'Maxi's Slave' across the front, one of my friend's T-shirts says 'Maxi's Butler', because he's the one who usually brings him food, and the other one says 'Maxi's Builder' across the front of his T-shirt, because he's the man who usually helps with building work in the sanctuary. Sometimes we show photos of Maxi the King working in his office, sitting at a desk with a computer, as if he's planning our workloads and the sanctuary's policies. He regularly complains about my car, saying he wants a Ferrari instead, and tells me I must get him one. When it's springtime, he orders me to plant flowers in his royal garden. We have an endless stream of jokes like this and people love it.

Maxi the King is very anti-cigarettes, though. I smoke a lot, especially when I'm angry or upset, and he tells me off because he doesn't like the smell. Maxi will knock my packet of cigarettes over and spill them all over the floor. He bosses me around all the time. He calls me 'slave Alaa' and opens his mouth very wide to shout his orders at me. With the cigarettes, he tells me he's noticed how I spend a lot of 'green kisses' – this is what we call our dollar bills – on my cigarettes. He says: 'Give me your packet of cigarettes immediately and I will break them all. In my kingdom smoking is forbidden. Now run and cook my meat for my lunch!'

Sometimes he complains about my cooking and shouts at me: 'Slave Muhammad Alaa Al-Jaleel, Servant Alaa, I'm sick of your kitchen's food . . . meat, meat, meat, every day. I want some tuna!!! Buy me some boxes of tuna for my royal body and my wonderful fur!'

When we need more funds for our projects, it's always Maxi who announces it. He says things like: 'Hello Fans, my new kingdom is almost ready! My subjects are arranging the doors, flowers, kitchen, the gym, and my personal beauty centre for my wonderful fur. But they need to reach the fundraising's goal to finish. Can you help?' Then we add a link to the donation page so that people can donate straight away.

Maxi offers us all an opportunity to have some fun. Of course, when we want to put something serious on Twitter, we usually do it differently. But Maxi is the most famous cat in the cat sanctuary. We submit to his authority as the ruler of his kingdom. He is the king of all the cats.

*

But, even with Maxi's leadership, it wasn't easy to launch the new sanctuary. My life was at risk. In the new sanctuary, the main danger was the threats from thieves, not from bombs. Local thieves tried to steal our funds after they discovered that huge sums of money had arrived for me, but luckily some other friends protected me. I defied the thieves and told them that, if I was scared, I would have left Syria a long time ago, but I'm not scared. I'm very proud of what I'm doing. I told them: 'You can't hurt people like me because I'm protected by people's love of me.' The thieves asked me for a large bribe in exchange for letting me work on the project, but thank God my civilian friends in the area volunteered to protect me and the project. Without them, I might not have been able to complete everything successfully.

To celebrate the opening of the new children's play-ground, which we built beside the sanctuary, just as we had in Aleppo, I organized a big party and invited about 300 children. It was the time of Eid, in June 2018, so we distributed gifts and sweets to the children and everybody was very happy, including the parents in the area, most of whom were internally displaced people like me.

This second sanctuary is a lot more developed than the first Ernesto's. It even has 'cathouses', which are not common here in Syria. This is all thanks to my Facebook friends, who suggested the idea. The design is like a small kennel for each individual cat, side by side round the courtyard of the villa, and each house has a white gabled roof carved with the name of the donor from the Facebook group. People here in Syria have never seen anything like these cathouses before and they like them very much.

This new sanctuary is also bigger than the original one and we follow a new system of feeding and caring for the cats. Soon after building the new sanctuary, we met a vet. His name is Mohammad Youssef. He was happy to work with us. We brought many new cats to the sanctuary, and among them were some who were ill, or others who'd been injured, usually because they'd been hit by cars. The doctor treated them and healed them. We also provided free health services for local people, as well as treating their animals for free.

We continued to have hard times during the fighting that sometimes broke out in the area between the militant groups. There was lots of infighting, which meant that sometimes we couldn't go out, as it was too dangerous, but we didn't give up. They're not usually in our immediate area, thankfully, but sometimes we still have to go through their checkpoints.

Once, I was stopped at a Jabhat Al-Nusra checkpoint while I was smoking and listening to songs on my radio. The guy who stopped me looked about sixteen, but he was armed. He put his hands on my car window – something I hate anyone to do – and told me that Imad Rami, the singer I was listening to, was a *kaafir*, an unbeliever, because he lives in the regime area of Syria and he takes money for his songs. I agreed with him straight away and turned my radio off. It's impossible to have a rational discussion with someone like this who's so ignorant. It was as if he'd only just left primary school, frankly. There's no security, only treachery, so it's best to leave them be and agree with whatever they say.

Then he told me that smoking was *haraam* and started to tell me off for that too. I agreed again and threw my packet of cigarettes out of the window. Luckily it only had two left inside. I've learned it's simply not worth having an argument with this kind of fanatic, so to save wasting time, and because I have to drive through that checkpoint most days, I just say what I need to in order to get along with him or any of them. He was so pleased that he came up and kissed me. Now we wave to each other each time I pass through, and he's very happy because he thinks he's converted me. One day I *will* quit smoking, when I am ready, but certainly not because of him.

★

These days I have two assistants who work with me at the new sanctuary, both of whom I'm close to and they help me a lot. This small, tight group suits me perfectly. All my life I never really had a big group of close friends. Since early childhood, I've never liked to go round in groups, and even now I don't like to go out at night with friends. I prefer to stay at home.

For nearly two years now it's been one of my daily tasks to search for stray cats that are in need of food or treatment. Some of the cats I've found stay in the sanctuary, but others come and go. Some cats often come back to get food, some come and go regularly, and others never come back. The number of our cats at the new sanctuary has reached about a hundred. We're taking good care of them. It's difficult to get medications and vaccines, but we're working hard and doing our best to get what we need from Turkey. We have to help these animals as much as we can.

In the new sanctuary we've also tried our best to carry on the work we used to do in the first sanctuary with local children, helping them understand the importance of animals, raising their awareness and showing them how to look after them. Just like in Aleppo, most of the kids in the neighbourhood here didn't like cats at first, but later, when they could see that the cats didn't hurt them, they liked them. Many children think that cats will scratch them, but the children in our neighbourhood soon became familiar with our cats. They got used to them. Now they come every day to play games and to sit with them and feed them, just like the kids did in Aleppo.

One day, some teachers in the area asked me if I could help their children to learn. It began by chance, because the manager of a local junior school had asked me to organize a party for their students. They have 120 kids, a lot of them orphans. We organized the party and it was a big success. The children like me very much and think of me as their uncle – sometimes they almost mob me when I arrive. And I liked the way the nursery was dealing with the children, so gradually we began organizing all sorts of other activities there too. We were able to convey the idea of animal welfare to the children. Most Syrian or Arab children will unthinkingly behave cruelly towards animals like cats and dogs, so we're trying to focus on this subject with them. We've developed a kind of pet therapy in what we are calling Gattaro's Kindergarten. It's very important to help a new generation of children grow up with respect and love for animals.

This was the same sort of work that we had started in the first sanctuary in Aleppo, and it makes me very happy that now, in the second sanctuary, it's developing again.

This school's initiative has allowed us to create a team of volunteers. In Aleppo we had two young women who were well educated, and we made them into a team, together with me and another young guy, so there were four of us. We used to visit schools every week in order to provide advice for kids on how to deal with animals. We raised awareness by holding sessions about how to, for example, deal with a cat that needs help or treatment or food. We explained that we must do what we can to help them, because most cats rely on people to feed them and there are many people who don't help these animals. We said: 'Tell your parents that you want to give cats any leftover food. Explain that you can put a plate of leftover food out in front of the house, rather than wasting it. Maybe a dog or a cat will eat from it.'

It was a great idea. The kids understood it and kept it in mind. They didn't forget. There were many children in Aleppo who did as we suggested. We also organized weekly trips for school students to come to the cat's playground. We explained to them how we feed cats and help them. If they saw a cat in the street, for example, we explained how they must first watch to see if the cat comes trotting towards them. If they do, this means the cat is ok and the child can go to it and stroke it. But if the cat screeches and stands still, it's better not to approach the cat. Maybe this cat had suffered a shock or been badly treated in the past. But even a cat like this could be helped by dealing with it from a distance. The children could feed the cat without touching it, just by leaving the plate of food outside for them. We taught them all sorts of things like that, both in the first sanctuary in Aleppo and again now.

We're known in the whole area round the second sanctuary now because we offer special services to children. We adopted all the same systems we used to have in Aleppo, so we coordinate with schools in the area to organize weekly parties and special events for children, where we give them food, sweets and toys and reward the best children at school.

We're also helping over a hundred families of orphans by giving them food and everything they need, thanks to the support of my friends from the Facebook group. It's our mission to show people how these animals have brought good luck for everyone. Through caring for animals I've been able to convey to people abroad the image of how much people inside Syria are suffering. People in the West know there are children and adults who need help via us, and we're expanding our activities day by day through our projects, which are designed to help both humans and animals. People have also started to bring us their animals to be treated at our new veterinary clinic as news of our resident vet's skills is spreading.

In my new life outside Aleppo, I have some friends here who fled with me after the siege. Other friends I have lost touch with, and I have no way of finding them again. For example, there was a little girl called Sedra who was often with us. She was ten years old and she was one of the children who fed the cats with me. She was going blind, poor girl, and her teeth also needed orthodontic treatment, so one of our Facebook group friends decided to help her, and the group continued to send her money for treatment and medicines. She had trouble seeing and had begun to lose her sight in one eye, as her retina was dying. My Facebook friends paid for the surgical operations for her eye which improved her sight by about 50 per cent, and for her teeth also.

Sedra had lost her father, and was living with her mother and two younger brothers. Her father had died, not because of the war, but because of a heart attack when he was only thirty years old. He'd worked in a workshop spraying cars, and the doctors said that maybe he'd been badly affected by the paint fumes. We were shocked by that, by how young he was.

This little girl had lived in the same neighbourhood as me, and she used to come to me regularly, bringing her friends with her, to help with feeding the cats. She visited the cat sanctuary almost every day. She liked the kittens especially, and used to spoil them by cleaning their eyes with wet wipes. She learned this technique from us.

But I don't know what happened to Sedra when we had to leave Aleppo. I lost touch with her, and I never had her phone number. Everyone got separated, so I don't know where she and her family are now, in which area or even in which country. I pray that Sedra and her family are ok.

One of the children from those Aleppo days who we're still in touch with and continue to help is Ibrahim, the son of Abu Ward, the 'last gardener of Aleppo', as the news channels called him. His name means 'Father of the Roses'. People used to go to him to buy flowers for their families' graves or for their own gardens, and we used to go there to buy plants and trees for our cat sanctuary and playground.

It was a very simple place, but Abu Ward joked to the journalist who interviewed him in summer 2016: 'My place here is worth billions of dollars. I own the world! We ordinary people own the whole world! The world is ours.' I knew exactly what he meant. The danger in which we lived had heightened our sense of life, our sense of community, the intensity of our feelings. Everything had become elemental. Nothing was taken for granted. Every last little thing was appreciated in a way that was very special.

Abu Ward was very proud of his son. 'My son Ibrahim is like gold,' he said. 'He's my special one. He stands here and the barrel bombs fall around him all day and he is not afraid. Death is nothing. For the faithful, God decides . . .'

In the intense bombing under the siege, when the regime and the Russians were trying to force a surrender, Abu Ward's plant nursery was hit by a barrel bomb dropped from a helicopter and he was killed outright. He'd always said he would be happy to die among the beauty of his flowers and he got his wish. Ibrahim was with him, and was knocked unconscious from the blast, but not physically injured. He was only thirteen and had left school to help his father. They were very close and used to spend hours together every day tending the plants.

For Ibrahim, his father's death felt like the whole world was gone. The garden centre closed. He had no idea what he would do now. At first he was full of revenge and bitterness and just wanted to kill whoever had killed his father. But just weeks later, the city fell and Ibrahim was forced to leave the city like the rest of us. He left on one of the green buses. From the news reports we learned that he ended up in a place twenty miles away to the west, a place called Daret Ezzeh and that his family had fallen apart after his father died. Alessandra, when she heard about his predicament, asked me to try to find him and see if he needed any help. It turned out to be a very complicated business, because Ibrahim and his sister Seba were orphans, and they were caught up in tensions between various sides of their family. Ibrahim and Seba were living with their uncles, and poor Seba had fallen ill since their father's death, because, like Ibrahim, she was very close to him and had been badly traumatized by his death. I went to see them, and took them to their father's grave. We planted flowers round his tomb.

I offered to help reopen his father's plant nursery so that Ibrahim could carry on his father's work, but his stepmother didn't want me to. She was afraid, because he was the eldest son and, if anything happened to him, there'd be nobody to look after them all. Her own son was only five, and her daughters were just six, seven and eight years old. Aleppo was still not safe and his road to work every day would be dangerous. So I helped them as best I could in other ways, buying them new clothes at Eid and mobile phones so we could stay in touch with each other. I visited the stepmother and the other children in the camp where they lived from time to time as well and brought them things like a washing machine, cooking gas cylinders and a bicycle. The last I heard from them was that they'd been moved to a new camp with proper buildings instead of just tents and were ok.

There were other cases like Ibrahim's where journalists and news channels got hold of these 'human interest' stories and then they went viral, read all round the world. They liked stories to do with children especially, because they knew there's always a big appetite for kids' stories. Bana Al-Abed, the little seven-year-old girl who posted on Twitter about the bombing in Aleppo, became famous acci-dentally because her tweets were in English – her mother had helped her – and this caught people's attention. But their story was then exploited by the Turkish government, staging photographs with Bana, smiling for the cameras once safely inside Turkey, to show off to the world how kind and merciful they are. She and her family got straight across the border at Bab Al-Salam to enter Kilis in Turkey, because special arrangements were made for them. But Bana is just one of thousands of little girls who were stuck under the bombing, only not all little Syrian girls have her international profile.

Others seeking the same route as Bana and her family were paying upwards of US$3,000 in bribes to Turkish border guards to get across. Urgent medical cases were still allowed to cross in ambulances like mine, though, so I often took badly injured people to the hospital in Kilis. The Turkish border officials used to make out a special permission form for the ambulance to say it was allowed to stay for one hour before it had to return to Syria. But people who needed treatment that wasn't life-threatening – things like bone grafts, which couldn't be done inside Syria – had to wait months on the border on the small chance they'd be allowed to cross. Turkey had been involved in the negotiations for the truce that ended the siege in Aleppo and the deal had been that injured people would be taken there. But with so many cases – over 3,000, because these were all the people injured in Aleppo over the last five months of the siege – they changed their mind and only let the urgent cases cross. They left the others at the border. Many of them died waiting there for months on end.

A friend of mine called Yasser Abu Muhammad who also had an ambulance, lost his leg while he was rescuing people and was among those trapped in limbo. He was stuck a whole month at the border getting documents and papers, until they finally gave him the approval to cross. He booked himself into a hospital and the doctors had to amputate his leg above the knee, even though his injury had been below the knee. Because he had to wait so long to cross, it had become infected, so the doctors had no choice but to cut it off higher. They gave him an artificial leg to use and he still suffers a lot every time he moves. When I'd crossed into Turkey myself to meet Alessandra and to see my family in Istanbul, I had to pay a US$2,500 bribe to get smuggled over. That was just how it was in December 2016.

There was another little boy, Kareem, who lost his eye and part of his face in the bombing of the Ghouta near Damascus in spring 2018. His story spread and became famous, capturing the imaginations of people far and wide, who posted pictures of themselves on social media with a hand over their eyes in tribute to him. When his family was displaced from the Ghouta in March 2018, the Turkish Red Crescent looked everywhere for him, essentially wanting to buy him so that he could be brought to Turkey for a photo opportunity, just like Bana. His family tried to hide him in a suitcase, but he was found and traded to them. The boy was taken to Turkey for a posed photo, but his family refused to go too and participate in the publicity stunt unless their whole extended family, fifty-three people in total, were also allowed to cross into Turkey. His family was very clever to do this.

The Last Sanctuary in Aleppo

The story of these children made me very angry. I swear by God, it seems there is not a president in the world, or a government, who really cares about people. They only care about their image and their interests. I hated the way these children were used, the way they and their families got privileged treatment and even got given Turkish nationality. They are protected now, while thousands and thousands of other children are left behind in the war zones. They need help just as much, but they are not famous, so no one cares. I consider all these children who stayed behind as if they were my own children. I take care of as many children as I can in my area, because I know what they've been through in this ugly war.

Today in the new sanctuary we have all the same programs as we had in Aleppo. Lots of children come to visit us and learn a lot from watching the cats. It's a very special thing that a cats' sanctuary is helping to take care of kids and also helping them to learn how to take part in the care of cats in return. It's such a privilege to be able to bring children to the cat sanctuary and to educate them like this. Schools come to us, and many local children ask their parents if they can have their birthday parties at our cat sanctuary. We always make them a special cake. It's a sanctuary for everyone – animal or human.

12: Faith and Football

People who live in the area know there's a cat sanctuary here, so they often bring me cats they've found. The cat sanctuary had been open about six months when two children brought me a little black cat, only three months old. They told me they'd found him in the street, hardly moving at all. I looked closely and found that he had gone completely blind in one eye, and that he could only see a little out of the other. I thanked the children and gave them some toys, which made them very happy, so, from that point on, whenever they found a stray cat they always brought it to me.

In Syria, many people particularly dislike black cats, because they believe that they are a *jinni* or a devil. Your word 'genie', in fact, comes from our word '*jinni*', which is a kind of spirit, usually evil. People are unsettled, I think, by not being able to see black cats in the dark. Most people, I'm sorry to say, will try to beat them or kick them away. Poor black cats – no one likes them, because they believe they may cause harm, like a devil in disguise, which is pure superstition. The flesh of a black cat is also said to protect against bad magic, although Islamic tradition stipulates that it is forbidden to eat the flesh of a cat. The only exception I know of was during the 'starve or surrender' siege of Homs in 2014, when all the poor residents were trapped there and, after years of starvation, they were slowly dying of malnutrition and reduced to eating grass, so the imam issued a *fatwa* – this is what we call a special religious judgement – giving special permission for cats to be eaten. Otherwise cats are protected, but I'm afraid there are still lots of false and damaging stories about black cats.

So we cleaned this poor little black kitten's eyes, washed him and gave him some food until, slowly, he became more active. A friend suggested calling him Fadi, after a friend who had died. Fadi has now been at the sanctuary for about a year. He's a very quiet cat. If we don't bring him food, he doesn't go and take it, but, because he's a blind cat, we're taking especially good care of him. He tries to play a little with the other cats, but it's hard for him. It's sad, because cats can generally see very well, much better than us humans, and can even see in the dark, because their eyes have very big pupils, but poor Fadi can't do any of this. The other cats seem to understand, though, and don't attack him for his weakness.

We try to play with him to ensure he moves a bit and gets enough exercise, because we're afraid he may grow weak. These days he's much better than before, and is starting to move more, but still not as much as a cat that can see properly. We continue to bring the plate to him, though, so he can eat, because otherwise he can't see the food.

Later on, we brought another black cat to the sanctuary. One of my Facebook friends adopted him and called him Shadi. It's an Arabic name, and they chose it because it sounds like the English 'Shady', in reference to his dark colour. Soon after that, we brought another black kitten back to the sanctuary and we called him Rodriguez. The incredible thing about Rodriguez is that he too is blind in one eye, just like Fadi. Now they all go round together and we call them 'the black gang' or even 'the black panthers'. They aren't a family, but they seem to have decided to be. It's funny how the black cats stick together. Sometimes the other cats don't want to play with the black cats, and Fadi and Rodriguez can't play much anyway because of their blindness, but Shadi always wants to play, so he makes funny movements and tries all sorts of antics, to trick the other cats into playing with him.

Alessandra and some of my friends in the Facebook group told me that studies have been done, genetic studies, that show that all pet cats are descended from wildcats from around 12,000 years ago, who lived in this part of the world, the Near East – the area that's now divided between Syria, Lebanon, Jordan, Israel and Palestine. Then, gradually, farmers made friends with them, until some of them started to live inside people's houses and become pets. But most of them still keep their ancestor's hunting habits. A cat like Fadi would have died in the wild, because he couldn't have hunted to feed himself. The interesting thing, however, is that the other cats are often kind and gentle with him, which isn't what you might expect. I often wonder how it would been if we hadn't rescued him, whether other cats would have looked after him. I think they might well have, as he wouldn't have been a threat to them and wouldn't steal their food.

I heard a nice story from my grandparents about this sort of thing, which backs up my theory. It was about a cat who lived on the city rooftops. Two men were eating their lunch on the roof of their local mosque and, as they ate, they fed morsels of their food to a cat as she passed. The cat took the food, ran off, and then soon came back for more. After the cat had done this several times, the men were curious to find out where she was going with this food, and so they followed her over the rooftops. They discovered that she was taking the food to a particular house and they watched as she laid the morsels of food carefully in front of another cat. This other cat was blind, they noticed. She couldn't catch her own food, so the other cat was looking after her.

We can learn much about love and tenderness from cats. I've seen how they show this love and tenderness to each other, and to cats that are disabled or injured in some way, but they also show this same love and tenderness to humans too. If they feel safe with you, they get very close to you and make you feel that they like you very much. Cats can sometimes fight amongst each other for food – that's their hunting instinct kicking in – but their relationship with people is different. They can help us to feel better and to relax if we feel upset and sad. I've experienced this many times myself and seen it happen with other people, especially children. Whenever I give food to any cat, I feel happy. When a cat comes to me and sits beside me, it makes me so happy that I forget my pain. Sukhoi 25, for example, if I call him, jumps straight up onto my shoulders. That makes me laugh and I forget whatever might be bothering me. I've seen the same thing again and again with young children, children who've been traumatized by bombing and the things they've seen. When they see a cat and the cat lets them stroke her or him, their mood lifts instantly. You can see it clearly in their faces and in the way they behave. It's a beautiful thing to watch.

★

We've recently had Ramadan, the eighth Ramadan since the war began. Of course the cats don't know it's Ramadan, and we give them the food exactly the same as normal, at the usual times, otherwise they would get very confused, but for us Ramadan is important: all our daily habits change during Ramadan.

In Islam, Ramadan, the ninth month in the Muslim

calendar, is our special holy month and lasts for thirty days, a complete lunar cycle. It starts when the new moon can first be seen, then ends approximately thirty days later, when the moon has waxed and waned and another new moon can again be seen. This month of fasting is one of the Five Pillars of Islam, and we only eat or drink after sunset during this time. It's difficult, of course, especially now, when Ramadan falls at the hottest time of year. Because it follows a lunar cycle, the month of Ramadan moves forward by about eleven days every year. When the war began in 2011, Ramadan started on 1 August, so for the last eight years, as it's gradually moved earlier in the year, the month of fasting has coincided with the hottest times of year. But, if you are ill or travelling a distance of more than eight kilometres, you're excused from fasting, and children usually don't start fasting for Ramadan until they're about ten or eleven years old. Before that, from the age of about seven or eight, children often fast just a few hours a day, to get used to it and to train themselves. This is how I was taught to do it. Like most kids, I began by fasting just at the weekend, not on schooldays, and just for three or four hours. We were happy to do it, because we wanted to do the same thing as our parents and to make them proud.

Ramadan is a very big thing and helps bring the community together. If you want, you can also give food or money to poor people instead of fasting. The amount you give is supposed to be equal to the price of a meal for one person, so in Syria this year it's US$1 a day, and in Lebanon it's US$5 a day. Many people pay it all in one go for the whole month.

It's not the fasting from food that is the hardest part. Much tougher is not being allowed to drink water or any kind of drink, hot or cold, from dawn until sunset. Also, for those who smoke, like me, that's the hardest thing of all. Any kind of smoking – cigarettes, cigars, pipes or water-pipes – what you call *shisha* – is also totally forbidden during daylight hours.

So, every evening at sunset during Ramadan, when the call to prayer or the cannon firing finally signals the exact moment to break the fast – *iftaar*, as we call it – everyone is already gathered together and waiting. Some people get carried away, and end up eating, drinking and smoking too much, but Ramadan is about discipline. As a boy, when I was feeling very disciplined, I would even give my *iftaar* breakfast to stray dogs and cats in the street and then break my own fast with just three dates, eaten slowly and thankfully. Ramadan gives us the chance to feel the hunger of others, to feel their pain. It helps us to feel closer to God and gives us the chance to help other people. It's the conclusion of the whole year for us, the climax, the best part.

This Ramadan, in the new sanctuary, I didn't go out much. I stayed most of the time alone, getting some rest and thinking about my life. I recited the Quran and I read it very carefully, trying to grasp its meaning. Sometimes it takes me a long time to understand one phrase. It's a

Muslim habit in Ramadan to read the whole Quran, but I prefer to understand what I'm reading rather than to read it fast without understanding. I also sleep a lot during Ramadan, and I listen to the Quran on my phone or on the radio before going to bed, which gives me a peaceful feeling. Sometimes I go to the special night prayers at the mosque, sometimes I do them at home. My relationship to God changes a lot during Ramadan. I think about God and what it means to be human and to be alive.

Since Ramadan in 2017, when it ran from late May until late June, here at the new sanctuary we've been offering people, especially orphan families, food and even ready-made meals. I concentrate on helping the orphan families because I can't afford to help all the poor people who need it and I feel there are other charities that are doing that. I'm most interested in helping widows and orphans, because I know they are the ones who need it most.

So, every day before *iftaar*, we prepare meals, rice and bread, then we give each family its share. Sometimes we add fruits or sweets for the children. I buy food every day for the cats and the animals in the sanctuary, and for those families as well. We're doing our best to help them all.

Also during Ramadan, from time to time we organize a collective *iftaar* and invite lots of people to come together to share the experience with one another. We all wait until the exact time of sunset, then we all break our fast together and share the first special moment where we taste food again and feel the water soothing our throats again after the hardships of the day. We feel closer to God in these moments and truly appreciate what we've been given. Organizing these collective *iftaars*, though, is a lot of work and takes a lot of preparation. There are only a handful of people working at the sanctuary, as we're a small charity, but we're very proud to be able to do this sometimes. Frankly, it depends on our financial capabilities. Sometimes, if we can't afford it but we have extra vegetables and fruits, we distribute them to people instead.

It's not just me who does this kind of thing. In Ramadan all Muslims are meant to give special charity to the poor, especially at *Eid al-Fitr*, the special festival at the end of the thirty days of Ramadan. Charitable giving, for which we have a special word in Arabic, *Zakat*, is a very important part of Muslim culture. That's when we give what we call the *Zakat Al-Fitr*, which means the charity of the breaking of the fast. The amount people are meant to give to the poor as *Zakat Al-Fitr* is equivalent to the price of three kilogrammes of dates, according to tradition, and the Ministry of Awqaf (Religious Affairs) in each country is responsible for deciding the recommended minimum sum. Of course this sum will be different from country to country, depending on their local prices and currency, but the principle is the same in every Muslim country. A father has to pay the amount on behalf of his wife and each of his children and give it to poor people, and it should be given any time after the middle of Ramadan, so that people can spend it to buy things for Eid. *Zakat* is another one of the Five Pillars of Islam, but I don't think people in the West hear much about these charitable practices that we have here.

It's also traditional for children to receive money as a gift for Eid. In Arabic this is called *Eidiyeh* and children collect this money from all their relations and then spend it during the days of Eid. Of course orphans who have no parents to give them these things normally get nothing. Thanks to my friends in the Facebook group, I've been able to help people like this, people in need, both adults and children, for the last two years, and especially during Ramadan. On the twenty-seventh night of Ramadan, we have a very special night called Lailat Al-Qadar. It's a very holy night, a night that most people spend in their local mosque, because it's the night on which we believe, by tradition, that our Prophet Muhammad received his first revelation of the Holy Quran, which we believe to be the actual words of God. This Ramadan, on Lailat Al-Qadar, we prepared 2,500 meals for people. We were also very busy preparing new clothes for orphans and widows.

Thank God I have found a way to be a bridge between people in the West and people here who need help. My friends in the West are very kind and generous; they like to help us and they are standing by us. Because of the hardships of war, people can't survive without help from abroad. Many men can't find work to support themselves and their families, and many families have lost their menfolk anyway. It's not like it used to be when I was a child, when most people could find work easily. It's very much harder now and everything has changed.

Some extremist people criticize me for accepting aid from the West. They tell me: 'The West is the cause of our problems, so how can you accept their help? Isn't it American planes and coalition countries like France and others who bomb us and kill our children?' But I tell them that this isn't true. The people in the West who I deal with are not the cause of our problems and are not responsible for the policies of their governments. Governments have their own interests, after all, which are different from people. I tell them that there are many people in the West who like us and who cry for us and pray for our safety. I say to them: 'Don't confuse governments with people. People in the West care a lot about us. They stand with us and are always ready to help.'

If we love each other, we should all live in peace. Look at us Muslims – we are fighting each other and among each other just because of different sects even though we share the same religion. It's so sad. We must help each other. My aim in life is to convey this message, that we should all live in peace. I have people from Israel who help me, and they want to create a similar project there, to make an animal sanctuary, in Haifa. It doesn't matter whether they are Jews or Palestinians. All that matters is that they are good people. We should be like a big multicultural community, where it doesn't matter what religion or ethnicity people are. We can all share one humanity and a love of weaker creatures.

I sometimes wonder if the cats notice things are different during Ramadan, if they can sense the different atmosphere. Ramadan is a time when families and communities come together, sharing the experience. Our cats are with us in the community every day, always eating together, so maybe every day is like an *iftaar* for them, who knows? For Fadi, as a blind cat, I think he notices something is different in Ramadan. He senses it, because his remaining senses will be stronger.

Another cat with very special sensitivities is Taaloub, which mean 'little fox' in Arabic. I called him this because he's ginger and white and his tail looked like that of a little fox once he grew bigger. He's one of the few cats that was with me in the old sanctuary, and he was brought back to me by one of the families from my Hanano neighbourhood. He'd been smuggled out of Aleppo with them on one of the green government buses in a vegetable crate. I originally found him in the streets of Aleppo, when we were under siege, and took him back to the cat sanctuary. He was so small, but he used to follow me wherever I went. At that time the cat sanctuary in Aleppo was being bombed with chlorine gas. The whole area was being heavily attacked, and when this cat saw me running away to higher ground to avoid the gas, he followed me to shelter. That's how he survived. It's as if he sensed I was going to a safe place. He's one of my favourites, the lucky one. In the West I think you say cats have nine lives – in Syria we say they have seven. Maybe this is because it's more dangerous here in Syria, so their life chances are fewer. But for Taaloub, it's as if he has a special kind of luck.

Taaloub is always kissing me, licking my face. He likes kissing. If I'm honest, he likes kissing most people, so I'm not so special. When anyone comes near him, he'll immediately give them a kiss. He loves to be close to people and always wants to sit on my lap, so he spends most of his time in the sanctuary these days. He doesn't leave it and he doesn't like to go out into the street, probably because of what he suffered in Aleppo. He's content to enjoy himself in the garden of the sanctuary, where he feels safe, playing football with wool balls and other things. I love this cat a lot.

Inspired by Taaloub's footballing talent and his special luck, I decided to see if he could predict the winner of the 2018 World Cup in Russia. Before each match I put out two dishes of meat for him, each one with the flag of whichever two countries were playing each other. Then we'd all watch to see which one he ran to and started eating from. That one was the predicted winner, and we filmed him and put it on our Twitter feed. His predictions were amazing – 90 per cent accurate at the start! We called him our 'Ginger Foxy' on Twitter and he gave his 'purrdictions' in a very amusing way, which people loved. As soon as I put him on the ground, he'd run towards one or the other bowl of food. He didn't hesitate. He made his decision very fast.

He got it right with the England v. Columbia match – he chose England. We were worried, because it was all decided right at the end, in the penalty shoot-out, and so we were all on the edges of our chairs, but he got it right, even though everyone was afraid England would lose at the end, because they hadn't won a penalty shoot-out before in a World Cup. We put out a tweet showing the pictures of him eating from the bowl with the England flag, the white one with the red cross of St George, to celebrate. Did you know, by the way, that the English patron saint, St George, was a Syrian soldier born back in Roman times? He's buried in a church in Ezraa in the south of Syria, and the church, which is called Saint George in his honour, is still used by the local Christians in the town there. Anyway, Taaloub chose the English bowl, and completely ignored the bowl with the Columbia flag.

We were rather surprised when he chose Belgium instead of Japan, but it turned out he was right about that too. And we knew it would be a challenge for him to choose between Belgium and Brazil on 6 July, and then between England and Sweden on 7 July, in the quarterfinals. It turned out that he got so stressed about all the pressure that we had to get another cat, Sparky, to take over the responsibilities for the final matches instead. Unfortunately, Sparky just didn't have the same flair for it, and didn't get any predictions right. So, for the actual final, we decided to spread the responsibility and get lots of cats to choose between France and Croatia. We even persuaded Maxi the King to take part, but he chose Croatia, and all the others followed his lead, so obviously none of the cats had any psychic powers after all.

★

However, most people in Syria found it hard to watch the 2018 World Cup. Not just because of electricity shortages or because they don't have enough money to pay for sports TV subscriptions, but because it was all being held in Russia. In Idlib Province, there are lots of former professional football players who were forced to stop playing by the regime, and hundreds of thousands of others lost their arms or legs in Russian airstrikes, but they still carry on playing the game they love – all through the war in Aleppo, children kept playing in the streets whenever they could in breaks between the bombing.

I even had some cats that were named after football teams: Manchester, Barcelona, Real Madrid. Some of my friends liked nothing better than to sit and chat about sport, so I named these cats for them, after the teams they supported. Syrians have always loved football, but we don't like to watch our international football heroes playing in

Russia, the country whose government is basically occupying our country, the country whose air force is in our skies, waiting to bomb us while we're cheering the games in their expensive stadia. It's a surreal feeling, the mix of bitterness and frustration. Sport should be a celebration of sportsmanship, bringing nations together. But while Russia was hosting the World Cup – the world's biggest sporting event – it was also bombing hospitals in Deraa, where I did my military service, and its support for the Assad regime has displaced more than 270,000 people in southern Syria. It's such a contradiction – at the same time as Russia is occupying Syria and committing war crimes against its people, it's also being praised and celebrated in the world media as an excellent host. But we won't let them take away our love of football.

13: Magic Zoo

Although most of our work at our new sanctuary is for cats, we do also offer help to other animals, according to whatever needs arise. Some of the cases are rather extraordinary. I'll start by telling you about our horse. He's called Ezel and belonged to a family near the city of Hama, south of Aleppo on the Damascus road. The family had been displaced more than once. They moved from village to village. One of my friends told me about this horse and about how much he suffered. Whenever the family was forced to move, they tied him up with a rope to their truck and drove with him like that, pulling him along. The family used their truck to transport their furniture, so there was no space for the horse in the back.

I met the owner of the horse and he told me that he couldn't help the horse any more. He didn't have a stable or anywhere to keep it, so I offered to buy it from him. I told him to give me a price and I'd pay him and then take over the care of the horse. This horse, by the way, is an Arabian thoroughbred horse. These kinds of horses are rare in Syria, because of the war, and so we're trying to save them. After I bought him, the owner gave me the horse's documents, including the horse's passport; these papers are made by the Ministry of Agriculture, to show he's an authentic Arabian horse. His parentage is given in the papers, his bloodline, which shows that his father was called Bibers. This horse has more documents than a Syrian person. In comparison, our ID card is very small just with our parents' names and our place of birth.

Horses need someone who understands them, so I found a man who's an expert in horses. He used to work at a stable with similar thoroughbred horses. Now he's displaced and lives with his family in an old broken-down house with a fenced field round it, so we pay him a small salary and he looks after the horse for us. Ezel was very neglected and thin because of the war at first, but now he's recovering well thanks to this man. He is always galloping around in his field, full of energy and life again, thank God. He's a beautiful brown Arab thoroughbred, very special in the way he moves. I don't have enough space for him at the sanctuary, but I plan to buy a piece of land close by where I can bring him. There are so few thoroughbred horses left inside Syria now that I worry about finding him a mare to breed with. I plan to perform the role of a traditional Syrian mother and try to find him a wife, so that he can have children and start building the population of thoroughbred horses up again in Syria.

Our monkeys are luckier. They're already a couple and are called Saeed and Saeeda. We found them when we were distributing aid in one of the camps for internally displaced people inside Syria. We noticed them in a small cage, just ninety centimetres high by fifty centimetres wide. It was a very tiny space for monkeys, and they were forced to stand in their own excrement, so the cage was very dirty and smelly. Their owner said: 'I don't have enough space for them. They were in a room in a house, but the house was destroyed and we were displaced, so I had to put them in this cage.' So I bought the pair of monkeys off him, and brought them to the children's playground near my sanctuary.

I was happy to have saved the monkeys and we built a much bigger enclosure for them with trees inside. I did all this with funds donated by my Facebook friends, who supported me in this venture as they have in so many others. I told them about the two famous monkeys who used to be in Aleppo, in Al-Sabeel Park. They were the original 'Saeed and Saeeda'. Everyone in Aleppo knew those monkeys and knew the many famous funny stories about them, so we decided to call them Saeed and Saeeda in their honour.

There were many parks in Aleppo – 171 parks in total, according to a book about Aleppo I've seen – but among them were two that were the most popular: the National Park, which we call Al-Hadiqa Al-'Aama, and Al-Sabeel Park, where people used to go on Fridays, our holy day, to have picnics and spend the day out of doors, away from the urban area. Friday was the only day of the week that was a holiday, and people would take all their food and drink along with them, sometimes cooking kebabs with their own barbecues. The adults sat on the grass in the shade, while the children ran round playing in the sun.

The National Park was the biggest planted park in all of Syria, in the area called 'Aziziyeh, between the Muslim and the Christian areas, next to the main Sa'adallah Al-Jabiri square in Aleppo, named after one of our early prime ministers from the 1940s. The park was very beautiful, in a hexagonal shape, with the River Qweiq running through the green spaces, and it was given to the city in 1949 by the elected head of Aleppo Municipality, in the days when those in power were often altruistic. His relatives didn't want him to give the land away, but he ignored them: 'This land is the property of the city of Aleppo. My grandfather Nafi' Pasha got it as a gift from the Ottoman Sultan, and now I give it back to the people of Aleppo.'

The design was wonderful, with lots of fountains, trees and flowerbeds, along with statues of some of Aleppo's most famous poets, like Abu Firas Al-Hamadani. Everyone loved coming there to relax and take photos of each other in front of all the colourful backgrounds. It was badly damaged in the war, and now lots of displaced families are living there, doing their best to find shelter under sheets and blankets. The residents of the local mental hospital also found refuge here too after their building was turned into a military barracks. The whole area was close to the frontline and fiercely fought over by regime and rebels.

As children, our favourite thing was when we went to the little zoo in the smaller Al-Sabeel Park, which had monkeys, peacocks, rabbits and pigeons. It was a bit further out of the centre to the north-west. These two monkeys, Saeed and Saeeda, were very well known and people had a lot of fun with them, giving them food, juice, water and sunflower seeds, even, you may be surprised to hear, cigarettes. They liked the seeds and cigarettes best, especially the cigarettes, which they used to eat! People in Aleppo used to tell all sorts of jokes about these monkeys, comparing them with married couples arguing, for example, so they were very much part of Aleppo's folklore, the stories of daily life in the city. In the summer, people used to love to go to the green open spaces like these for the fresh air, because most didn't have any air conditioning at home. Only rich people had air conditioning. Al-Sanam (Statue) Park on the outskirts of the city was another favourite place where people would picnic under the trees, as well as Al-Hizam Al-Akhdar (The Green Belt) amusement park, with its restaurant and playground. A lot of these parks and playgrounds were either damaged in the war or badly neglected.

★

When we first brought the monkeys back to the sanctuary, they were very ill and thin. They had an infection around their eyes as well as around their necks, but after we took care of them, they recovered and got much better. They also became much more active and fast-moving. When I first built the big new cage, and I was just moving them into it, the male monkey, Saeed, bit me. It really hurt and left a nasty wound. But I didn't get angry. I realized that the reason he bit me was because he was afraid I might be trying to put him back into the tiny cage. He didn't understand I was trying to help him. It eventually took two of us to move the monkeys into the big new proper cage.

Now they live happily there, in the new Ernesto Sanctuary, eating the fresh fruit and vegetables we bring for them. Bananas seem to be their favourite thing and they perform all sorts of acrobatics on the ropes and swings we installed for them on the tree branches in their cage. Sometimes we post videos of them swinging around in their cage on our Twitter feed, so that people can see how well they're doing. They're quite young still, about fifteen months old, the vet tells me, and we're hoping they may even have children. We'd love to see a baby monkey, but so far it seems that Saeed doesn't know how to mate with Saeeda. She takes a lot of interest in him, but he doesn't pay any attention to her and doesn't seem to care. We joke that maybe he needs Viagra. When I go into the cage, they will take a banana from my hand, and Saeeda pulls my hair. Both of them have very human-looking eyes, which have the same expressions as we do. Saeeda often has a very aggressive look in her eyes, as if she's going to attack us. We're not frightened of her, but we're terrified of her eyes. When the children come close to their cage to look at them, if they're holding any food, like a bag of crisps, the monkeys are nimble enough to steal their food, because their hands are so slender they can reach through the holes from inside their cage and snatch things. The holes are tiny, just three centimetres by three centimetres, but their hands fit through, so they sometimes grab the kids' hair too. They're always larking about and making us laugh.

We also have a few white rabbits at the sanctuary. Their owners left them with us and asked us to take care of them and feed them. There are two males and one female and they've already had babies. They don't mix well with the cats, so we put them in the kids' playground. The children like watching them and playing with them there. We also have five pigeons, two ducks and three geese in the kids' playground, so the kids can interact with them too. When I bring the food for the monkeys, I also bring lettuce and carrots for the rabbits and the birds.

We have many skills between us at the new sanctuary. We have a man who works in the clinic – he registers the names of the patients and keeps the records – who now also takes care of the pigeons. He said to me: 'Don't worry, I'll take care of them.' He understands them and gives them food and water every morning. If they're ill, he can tell, and he also knows where to look to find their eggs.

We now have a little black pigeon chick, but not from the sanctuary's pigeons. He was brought to us by a little girl called Malak, whose father had been killed while he was out getting food for the family. He'd got caught up by accident in the local clashes between the rival groups and, by coincidence, on the very same day her father was killed, this black baby pigeon chick turned up at Malak's house. She kept it and we brought it to our playground to be looked after. She was afraid that if she left it alone, it might die, so she wanted it to be with the other pigeons. Imagine that, how a little girl can think that straight after her father has just died. It was little and couldn't fly, so she called me from her aunt's phone and said: 'I have a pigeon chick. Could you come and get it?' It's doing fine with the other pigeons now.

After the new sanctuary became well known in the area, a man called me and told me there were some animals in the Aleppo Magic World Zoo, including lions, tigers, hyenas and bears. He told me many of the animals had already died from hunger and from the bombing, and asked if I could help with the animals that were still left. I told him it was a bit difficult for me to help these kinds of animals. That really was beyond any of our skills. But for more than three months this man kept calling me, asking me to help. In the end I went to check the place and to see these animals for myself.

The place where the Magic Zoo is located was in a very dangerous area at that time, as it was on the Damascus road about fifteen to twenty kilometres south from Aleppo. It was in an area controlled by the fighters of Tahrir Al-Shaam, a group linked to Al-Qaeda, so it was dangerous for me to reach it. The man who contacted us had tried to speak to the regime about the animals, but when he'd contacted the Ministry of Agriculture in Damascus, they told him to contact Alessandra and Muhammad Alaa Aljaleel instead. They told him they'd heard that these people were looking after animals. It was funny that the Ministry knew about us and was handing over responsibility for the zoo animals to us. I'm sure they knew I went there after that to check on the animals.

When I arrived, I was shocked to see how many animals had died. The day I arrived the last of the deer had just died – there had been eight originally. There were also two tigers that were very sick. I took pictures of them and sent them to my Facebook friends, who then told me they would do what they could to help, first by consulting vets, then by sending money to feed the animals. They transferred urgent funds out to me so that I could buy the fresh meat the vets recommended, as, up until then, these animals had been living on waste food, mainly dead chickens, as there was a chicken farm next door to the zoo, and the guard of the zoo, the man who'd contacted me, used to collect dead chickens to feed the animals. About twenty animals had probably already died because of being fed these dead chickens.

In total there were four lions, seven jaguars, one bear,

two husky dogs, two hyenas and two tigers. I discussed the situation of the animals with the zoo guard. It turned out the actual owner of the zoo was living in the USA. I asked the guard why he kept calling me and what he expected me to do for these animals. He replied: 'I'm so tired. I've been feeding these animals now for four years. I need somebody else who can help me.'

Then he said that he wanted to sell the two tigers and the bear. I asked him: 'How are you going to sell two sick tigers? Nobody will buy sick animals. You can't sell them. You should help them instead.' Then he said that he wanted to sell them before they died. I asked him: 'Why don't you sell them all?' But he said that he wanted to sell just the tigers and the bear for US$20,000. I sent a message to my Facebook friends about this man's offer and they replied saying that they couldn't afford to buy the animals. They also said that it wouldn't be right to buy the animals from this man, since he didn't even own them – they were owned by the man in the USA. What my friends did say, though, is that they could afford to help buy food for the animals.

So I started to bring food for them. I told the man that I couldn't buy the animals but that I could feed them, and that we needed to contact the owner in the USA. I bought fresh meat for the animals like the vet recommended, but the man asked me to give him the money so that he could buy the food. I told him I couldn't give him the money, but I could buy the food and deliver it to him. I suppose he'd noticed that I was bringing a lot of food, so he thought he might be able to benefit somehow and take some cash for himself, but I told him that I alone was responsible for this money and that I couldn't give it to anyone else. Yet he carried on insisting that he should have the money and buy the food for the animals instead. I continued to refuse. Then the Four Paws Association called me and asked me how they could help. I told them to negotiate with the owner in the USA, and after long negotiations, they finally reached an agreement.

The Magic World Zoo gave me a lot of headaches. I was threatened because of it and there was an attempt to kidnap me. The kidnappers thought that, because I was buying a lot of food for these animals, I had a lot of money. They threatened me more than once, so in the end I decided to stay away. I spoke to Dr Khalil from the Four Paws Association and gave him the phone number of the owner, and then I left the vet who works with me to take care of the animals. It took them about a month to solve the situation of the animals. I heard they paid a lot of money to the owner in the USA and to the guard. The animals are now spread between Belgium, the Netherlands and Jordan. My Facebook friends still send me their pictures from time to time.

★

There's no other cat sanctuary in Syria apart from Ernesto's Sanctuary for Cats, but there used to be an animal reserve.

It was near Palmyra, south of the road east to Deir Ez-Zour, and it was called the Talila Reserve. It specialized in endangered species, especially the oryx, a large antelope with big straight horns which lives in the desert. Some people say it's the origin of the unicorn myth, because when you see it from the side, it looks as if it's just got one long straight horn. The reserve opened in 1992 and was the joint finance project of the Ministry for Agriculture, the Food and Agriculture Organization and the Italian government. It was an area with a perimeter fence of seventy-two kilometres and had 380 protected gazelle and sixty-five oryx. Not many people visited it, though, because it was difficult to get a special visitors' permit. During the war, rebels broke the fence and hunted the oryx and barbecued them. I was shocked to hear about this, and the lack of education and respect that went with it. In Syria the Ministry of the Environment is new, only a few years old, and in Syrian schools there's no education about the environment and the importance of animals, sadly.

When it came to birds, however, I heard that, before the war, there had started to be a few new initiatives to protect the ones in danger of extinction. In 2009, a group of young Syrian bird-lovers produced their own guidebook on the birds of Syria, to help children and adults recognize the different bird types and learn to respect them. They tried to introduce the guidebook in schools, printing it at their own cost and distributing it for free, but they had mixed success and a lot of resistance. God knows where these books are now. Most probably they've been burnt like firewood by people needing to keep warm in the cold winters, after they were forced to leave their homes to escape the fighting and bombing. Often people had to light campfires and sleep out rough in the open.

Some species of birds are under threat, of course, because many Syrians love to hunt and shoot birds. It's nothing to do with Islam. In fact, in Islam there are four months during which it's meant to be forbidden to hunt animals or to fight. These months are Muharram, Rajab, Dhu al-Qa'dah and Dhu al-Hijja, but not many people follow these rules.

The Caliph Umar, who's buried in Ma'aret an-Nu'man, south of Aleppo, and who was the second caliph after the Prophet Muhammad, had a famous saying encouraging people to look after birds. According to the *Hadith*, he said: 'Scatter grain on the mountains to feed the birds, so that people will not say that the birds went hungry in the time of Umar.'

South-east of Aleppo there's also a seasonal salty lake called Al-Jaboul, which was made into a special nature reserve before the war. Lots of water birds like flamingos stopped there on their migrations, and there were plans to try to bring eco-tourism bird-watching groups to the lake, and to convert the old Ottoman caravanserai, that used to store the salt, into a boutique hotel. The plan never took off because the Aleppo governor wanted too much bribe money. It was the usual story of greed and corruption.

In the forests behind Lattakia, there was also an area that was supposed to be protected called Furolloq. But because of the air strikes and the bombing of the forest – things which the Syrian regime did to force the rebel fighters out of their hiding places – there's been a lot of damage and forest fires that have damaged the pines, cedar and oak trees. I heard that some people have started to plant new trees. I hope it's true.

14: A New Normal

My daily routine in the new sanctuary is rather different to how things used to be before, in the old sanctuary under the siege in Aleppo. In the new sanctuary, I actually have a routine. I wake up every day between 8 and 9 a.m. The first thing I do is to feed the kittens. If there are no kittens, then I give the cats their food. Around noon I drive to the border to buy chicken meat, which is brought in from Turkey. Many things are brought in from Turkey to this part of Syria, not just food but all sorts of other things that we can't get easily in Syria anymore. If I don't go on time to bring the meat from Turkey, I would have to buy it from the black market instead, which is very expensive. But cats have to have meat. Without it they aren't healthy, as we discovered during the siege when they had to eat a lot of rice. They have trouble digesting vegetables and plants, because their gut is designed to process meat efficiently.

After I've bought the food I return to the sanctuary to prepare lunch for the cats, while they're having their veterinary check up, to make sure they're all healthy. Cats like their meat to be at 38 degrees, like a fresh kill. If it comes out of the refrigerator and is too cold, they reject it, because their instinct tells them it's been dead for too long and might not be safe to eat any more. All these habits go back to their origins as carnivores and hunters, and even after they've been pets a long time, these instincts are still there. These animals are our link to the wild and we need to respect them and their habits from those times.

After I've finished feeding them, I play with the cats. I like to see cats defending themselves. When I play with them, I like to train them to be strong. So I fight with them to make them defend themselves, in a kind of game, not for real. Sometimes they hurt me a bit by biting me, but only slightly, because they know I'm just playing with them. I feel very happy when I see that they're protecting themselves. It's good for them to do this, so sometimes I shout or roar at them like a lion or a tiger to see their reaction. I know from experience that they like best the person who's tough with them. For example, when I have a cat that beats up other cats, what I do is beat him up a little bit in return and play roughly with him. After that, he likes me a lot. We have two proverbs in Syria about this kind of thing, which maybe even explain a bit about what is going on.

The first one is: 'The cat likes the person who strangles him.' We use this to describe someone who, even after you do them a favour, doesn't treat you well, but instead is nice to people who treat him badly. It's a negative thing when it's about people, but maybe cats have learned that this helps them to survive better, if they are super tough. Certainly, in Syria, our tough environment during this war has maybe led people to behave more like cats these days.

And the second one is: 'He who wants to play with the cat must bare his claws.' This one is like a kind of warning, to someone who's perhaps risking more than he should, taking more risks than is sensible. Again, in Syria these days a lot of people are forced to behave like this, to defend themselves. In fact, when I think about it, I'm having to behave like this myself, taking lots of risks in order to set up my sanctuary, going against the local customs where animals aren't valued. Sometimes you have to be very tough and go against the flow to get things done.

After feeding the cats and playing with them, I often go to the junior school to see the children. This is our own school, which is funded through the cats' sanctuary. I love seeing the children and playing with them too. Then, from about 2 p.m. until 4 p.m., I go round and check on people in the neighbourhood, to chat with them and see if anyone needs help or anything else.

Then I go back to the sanctuary to prepare dinner for cats. That's a normal, regular day, but if there is bombardment or if there are clashes in the area, then of course I can't do all that, because I have to drop everything and drive off to do my ambulance and rescue work. Unfortunately, we're still not safe where we are. We're always in danger and there's always the risk of bombing and fighting. If that's the case, I leave one of my assistants in the sanctuary to take care of everything while I'm away.

It's still difficult to get diesel fuel, even now. I try always to have enough for the electricity generator, because we still don't have a regular electricity current. This makes things hard for us, as it also means we have no internet and are disconnected from the outside world. Water is also a big issue. We always bring it in a water tanker, a big truck full, and then every other day we fill our water tanks with about 5,000 litres. We use a lot of water, because we clean the sanctuary three times a day, after every mealtime. We do this as a precaution, to stop any disease spreading.

Sometimes when I have special events to supervise, like a kids' party at a school, I leave my assistant in the sanctuary to do my work instead. I've trained him to do the same things that I do, feeding the cats and taking photos of them to post on Facebook and Twitter. We post photos of the cats on Twitter every day and also on the Il Gattaro di Aleppo Facebook page. We send the photos to Alessandra, Lorraine and Jane, my friends, and they then post the photos and any news. Whenever I bring a new cat back, I always make a video so that our friends in the group can see it, as one of them might even want to adopt this new cat. The cats that I bring back are mostly strays that need help or treatment. We send daily news and photos of the cats to my friends in the group to keep them informed.

I do all these things for the group, as I feel happiest when I'm able to give pleasure and to help others, both people and animals. To be honest, I care much more about others than about myself. I've kept nothing for myself. People sometimes assume I must be a rich man from all the donations we receive. They think I must have shops or businesses in Turkey, but I own nothing. Even the villa and the farm of the sanctuary are in my children's names. I want them to continue this work after me. My target is to expand the sanctuary beyond the clinic and the playground we already have, to build a kindergarten, a centre for the disabled and an orphanage. We already deal with a lot of orphans in our area, but we do it discreetly. We don't post photos of this on social media, though, as, for a start, we can't take pictures of them with their female relations, most of whom wear the *hijab*, a headscarf that covers their hair. Europeans don't like to see photos of women in *hijabs*, I find. And some of the women may have relations in the regime-controlled areas and so don't want their faces seen. They would never ask for help, even the poorest ones never ask. Helping orphans is one of the biggest duties in Islam and it's mentioned many times in the Quran. It's very special work.

My cats give me the strength to do all this. Sukhoi 25 and Sukhoi 26 and Taaloub are the original cats from the first sanctuary that survived and are still with me in the new sanctuary. Unfortunately, Ernesto, the cat we named after Alessandra's cat, left the sanctuary two months ago.

We couldn't make him stay. Everyone was sad to see him go; we used to joke that he was like the Orange President of our Aleppo Sanctuary (once we had some fun with him and made his orange hair into a big tuft at the front to look like President Trump. He didn't like it much, but it was very funny). Like all male cats, when he reached full adulthood at two years old, he wanted to become independent and go and live his own life, just like I wanted to leave home and be independent when I was a young adult. Tomcats are like this. It doesn't mean that he has forgotten us, though, and he still comes back to visit from time to time.

Most of the time Sukhoi 25 and Sukhoi 26 stay inside the sanctuary, but sometimes Sukhoi 26 goes out, because originally he's a stray cat. He's very happy at the sanctuary, so he always returns. They're still as fast as ever, especially when it comes to food, and their names are still as suitable as before, because, even now in the new sanctuary, we still see the Russian Sukhoi jets overhead.

In Arabic our word for 'cat' is 'qitt', or 'qitta' for a female cat, so it even sounds like the English word. Maybe we even gave you this word from Arabic? The funny thing is that when you write the word 'qitt' in Arabic script, the shape even looks like a cat.

Our letter 'Q' looks like the cat's head with two ears as the two dots, the body of the letter 'TT' is like the cat's body with its legs tucked under as it lies on the ground, and the tail of our letter 'T' is like the cat's tail sticking up in the air.

But for tomcats we have another special word – we call them 'hirr', which is from our word 'to growl'. Cats have their territory that they roam, which can sometimes be quite small, just a few hundred metres from their home. But if they are wilder, they can roam over very large areas, even up to twenty-five hectares. We don't know how far he goes, it could well be that far afield, but Ernesto still comes occasionally to the sanctuary. When he comes we greet him like a long lost friend and are very happy to see him.

Male cats always fight, but some of the females live in peace with one another, much more than the male ones. I have more female cats than male ones. The only male ones I have apart from Shadi are Ernesto (when he's about), Firas and Manchester. They're all over two years old now, so they're fully adult and they're always fighting with each other. We call these tomcats '*haroun*' in Arabic. My Facebook friends have told me that the ancient Egyptians sometimes called Ra, their main sun god, the 'Supreme Tomcat'. Ra disguised himself as a huge cat, it is said, and fought against the darkness, which was in the shape of a huge snake. It was the fight of the Cat of Light versus the Snake of Darkness, a very ancient tradition. It's the fight we're still fighting today in Syria.

Thanks to the vet who now works with us, we're trying to get all our cats neutered. Apart from helping make the males fight less, it's actually much kinder to them too, I've learned. It helps them live longer and makes them healthier. In the wild they'd normally only live about seven years, but with medical attention and neutering they can live twice as long. The vet told me that neutering means the males can't get cancer of the testicles and the females can't get cancer of the uterus and the ovaries. So all that's a good thing. It's surprising how often cats do get cancer. That's how Alessandra's cat died, her Ernesto, the one she loved so much, after whom we named the sanctuary.

My friends in the Facebook group tell me that lots of pet-owners in the West and the rest of the world don't control the breeding of their pets as they should. Some people, even in the West, just abandon their cats and other pets when they don't want them anymore or can't look after them for whatever reason – maybe they moved from a house to a flat or lost their job or something like that? Apparently, they've told me, a financial crisis is very often the reason. They said that, after the big banking crash in 2008, lots of pets were abandoned all over the world.

When cats get pregnant, they usually give birth after a couple of months to three or more kittens. These kittens stay with their mother until they are weaned at around four months, and then, by the time they are six months old, they're fertile and the females can get pregnant themselves. What all this means is that there are now too many wild cats in the world. Wild cats are hunters, killing to eat. If you watch them when they're hunting, you'll see how good at it they are. They put each back paw straight into the space where the front paw just was, so that they leave few tracks and make very little noise, just like lions. They're so good at catching birds that lots of kinds of birds are at risk of extinction because there are too many wild cats in the world. This is why I started to think about how important it is to neuter the cats. It makes me think about all these things I never thought about before, but when I was little I just looked after all the cats I could find because I loved them and because my grandparents and parents taught me how.

In our clinic our vet also now gives all our animals treatments for parasites like worms and fleas, and gives them vaccinations to make sure they stay healthy. In Syria at the moment we have lots of diseases because of the war, and because so many doctors left and so many hospitals were destroyed. We cannot train new doctors. We don't have the facilities. But we can try to train a few people to help the doctors we still have at least. I myself learned a lot about injuries and diseases during this war, things I never knew before.

Last year TB spread in the sanctuary and many of our cats died from it. That was before we had the vaccines, so we couldn't protect them from it. We recognize it now and know that when a cat has TB it develops a white crust in the corner of the eye. It can't move and doesn't have the energy to stand up, then it dies within three days. We've learnt from what you do in the West and we've started to isolate any cases where a cat becomes ill, and to put them in a separate cage so that the infection or disease can't spread to the others. We also learned how important it is to feed them well to keep their immune system strong, especially with kittens that have lost their mother before they're weaned. We try to feed them human baby formula milk, to replace their mother's milk, but they don't like it. So we end up feeding them luncheon meat, tinned sardines or tuna instead, even though they are too young. Many people criticized us for feeding kittens with meat and solid food, but we tell them we're trying to help their immunity to diseases after they lost their mother's milk.

We're all learning new things because of this war. We have to do this, to survive. One incredible case we had was of a cat I found which had been badly injured. Her back legs were broken but otherwise she was a healthy cat. She'd probably been hit by a car. So our vet set her back legs and then we designed a kind of feline wheelchair for her. We didn't have any of the proper materials, but there was a plumber who was doing some work for us installing plastic water pipes. He saw the cat and suggested he could perhaps make something with the tubes. So he cut the tubes to the right length, helped by our vet, who knew how high it should be. Three men worked on this wheelchair, joining the tubes together with a special soldering iron. It was completely improvised, made from bits and pieces we found about the place. We made a special harness to hold the cat in place in the wheelchair, so that her weight at the back was supported. After all, cats cannot use crutches like humans when they have a broken leg or ankle, so we had to invent something new. Necessity is the mother of invention. We've invented lots of things in this part of the world – the phonetic alphabet, Arabic numbers, cheques and lots of scientific things like algebra. We even invented alcohol. Maybe it's because this part of the world has always been in turmoil, with unreliable rulers and incompetent states, so we had to rely on each other and on our own communities. At least that's what I sometimes think.

All our friends in the Facebook group were so interested in this cat with the wheelchair, how she would survive, how she would manage, whether she would learn to move about using this new wheelchair that we'd made especially for her. At first she didn't know how to move around in it, but after a day or two she succeeded. Unfortunately she didn't survive for more than a week or two, but her story had a lot of positive effects. We improved the wheelchair design and were able to help a lot of paralysed cats that way. People love to hear about ways of overcoming problems. It gives us all hope for the future, hope that we can manage somehow, no matter what fate throws at us. It brought our community closer together.

Epilogue: What the Future Holds

When I was young, I always wanted to help people and cats. I inherited these passions from my father, so it's in my blood. Even before the war, I always felt a thrill and a special happiness when I saw ambulances driving past with their loud sirens, because I knew it was people helping others. Humanitarian work makes me feel like I have a purpose. For some people the best thing may be the happiness they feel in worshipping their God, or the joy of their wedding day, but for me this joy is what I feel when I help or rescue someone, or extinguish a fire or do something useful to humans. I don't know why I've always had this feeling, why I love to help. For me it's just the best thing in life.

Of course I would never have wished for a war in order to make my dream come true. I wish I could've achieved these things without the suffering I have seen. My kids and my family all know that. God blessed me by putting me in a position where I could help people by being a rescue man, but in my worst nightmares I never imagined a war like this for my people or for my country, or even for a single animal. I never wished to achieve my dream in this way.

Many people have been killed doing this work, however. We regularly found ourselves in dangerous situations, but if we weren't killed, we grew stronger. I became stronger and I conquered my fear. If a shell landed next to me, I wouldn't run away. And when I saw that nothing had happened to me, I felt even more courageous. I was exposed to death more than a hundred times at least, but whenever the danger had passed I simply felt stronger, so I would return to the same place to help again and again.

At the beginning of the crisis in Syria, when the fighting first started in 2011, Aleppo was considered a safe place to go. People used to flee from the countryside outside Aleppo, which was being shelled, and they came into the city for safety. Many came from Homs when the Old City there was being bombed and its souks destroyed. Many people even came from Damascus, when the fighting and shelling first began there in the suburbs. They left the capital and fled to Aleppo for safety. It's hard to remember those days when I think about what happened at the end of 2016, the worst period we had in Aleppo, in those last days before the city fell. That was the tragedy that we lived through and somehow survived.

I believe that because I have always cared for other living things since I was a child, God helps me a lot, especially in my work. I always say to myself, and I know it is true in my heart, that the reason I have survived is because of the animals I'm looking after. They repay me this way, thanks be to God. In turn, thanks to these animals, God has helped me to help the other people around me. In Aleppo we bought ambulances, we dug water wells, we supported our neighbourhood of 2,000 people with food, water and electricity, we offered comfort and therapy to orphans and children in our cat sanctuary and playground, we ran animal care classes in schools and even helped lonely old Christians and Muslims in their homes. The support of my Facebook friends in the group who liked my humanitarian works helped me to do all of this and more.

My life has not been an easy one. Staying behind in Aleppo was my choice, but I didn't know how difficult it would be, and that my cat sanctuary would eventually be bombed as well. Throughout all the bombing, even in that final house where I lived in Aleppo, I had the cats with me and I had the support of God and my Facebook friends.

I believe that much of the work I do should be a government duty, not down to individuals, but in Syria we cannot count on the government. My project is huge and needs a lot of money and effort. We always knew the costs would be very high, but my friends said they would help wherever they could. They shared with others my hopes to build a new sanctuary and soon the members of my Facebook support group grew from 9,000 people to 20,000, people from all around the world. My Facebook friends are supporting me, and although we are facing many difficulties together, we're carrying on and we'll continue until we launch our future big projects, beyond the new sanctuary.

Thanks to the generosity and benevolence of these people, I was able to purchase land and a partially destroyed building in the countryside of West Aleppo Province. This is where we now have our new Ernesto Cat Sanctuary, Ernesto's Paradise, as we call it. We employed local people to help with the construction work, and built another playground, called 'The Playground of Hope: Pet Therapy for Children', named after Hope the dog who was fatally injured when our sanctuary in Aleppo was bombed. Local kids, children from refugee camps, and children made orphans by the war can now visit the cats and our other animals and play with them. When they come to us, it's like a therapy for what they've been through during these stresses of war, and they learn respect and love for animals as they play. We even have our own buses, which we bought with funds donated by the Facebook group, and these buses bring kids from local schools and orphanages to visit the sanctuary and the playground.

I thank God that as an individual I've been able to overcome all the difficulties of working on this project and that I am now surrounded by true friends who are helping me in my work. I trust them a lot. Among them is the vet who works with us, Muhammad Youssef. Finding a vet was very difficult, because most of them left the country, but like me, Dr Youssef stayed behind. Thanks to him, the sanctuary can now give free care for all the animals in the area, not just for the ones inside the sanctuary.

Whenever we can get hold of anaesthetics for the animals, Dr Youssef also now does operations to spay and neuter the cats. Anaesthetics are expensive and in short supply, so it will take us a long time to do this for our cats – and our dogs – but we know how important it is, to help them keep healthy and live longer lives. We're also trying to educate the local people about the importance of this. Thanks to all the generous donations, we've even been able to buy an ultrasound machine to help with diagnosis of illness. And we've bought more land next to the sanctuary in the hope of giving Dr Youssef a full-service clinic. The number of animals at the sanctuary has grown quickly. We now have around a hundred cats and kittens, lots of dogs, four monkeys, rabbits, doves, geese, and our horse.

We are a team now. Alessandra Al-Abidin, the creator of the Facebook group, has been a big support to me. She was able to explain the whole situation so well to people outside Syria. Thanks to Alessandra, who translated these thoughts and ideas to people in the West, we've managed to raise funds for people in Aleppo who were in need of help. It all began because some of the people in the group wanted to help people who couldn't afford to buy food for themselves, as they understood that people couldn't take care of animals if they couldn't even take care of themselves.

Epilogue: What the Future Holds

The original Ernesto's Sanctuary was very successful at helping people, and through this new sanctuary we've been able to help even more fellow Syrians. Alessandra has provided me with a link to the West and conveyed all the information about my work to people in Europe and elsewhere. We're so happy to have achieved all this. People in the neighbourhood of the old sanctuary and here in this area of the new sanctuary are really happy to get help from a cat sanctuary, especially when so many NGOs are unable to help people in Syria.

It seems the world cannot solve wars and conflicts these days. That's why there are now so many refugees around the world, but especially here in the Middle East. I do not want to be a refugee. I want to stay in my country, in Syria. I want to help people in any way I can. Everyone says the destruction of Aleppo was the low point in the war, that things will slowly get better. I hope they are right. But I still don't know what will happen to me and to the area where I live in north Syria. We are close to Aleppo but we are also very close to Idlib Province, where there's still a lot of uncertainty about the future. Most of us are civilians, but there are still some armed groups.

There is a lot of talk that because the regime and the Russians retook Deraa Province in July 2018, they will now make a final offensive to take Idlib back into their control. There's supposed to be a ceasefire, but the regime says Idlib is full of terrorists like ISIS and Jabhat Al-Nusra. Thank

God, in the area where the new sanctuary is, we don't have any extremist groups. But there are some close by, and the regime will probably use them as an excuse to attack the whole area, as they've done in all the other parts of Syria. Sometimes I have to go through their checkpoints, so I can see how ridiculous these extremists are, with their beards and guns. Many look as if they're only just out of primary school. But there are not many of them and they mainly fight each other.

Before the war I was just normal when it came to religion. I went to the mosque to pray, not to listen to the sermons. But after the war I distanced myself from religion. I learned from this crisis that many people use religion as an excuse. Even criminals became religious if it suited their purpose. Now I very rarely go to the mosque, because it's full of extremists pretending they understand religion. Everything was turned upside down by this war. People who knew nothing about Islam suddenly called themselves religious, and people who knew a lot were suddenly labelled *kaafirs* or unbelievers. I am religious in my own way, which is just between me and my God.

The world thinks we're terrorists, and a lot of this is because of the propaganda of the regime. From the very first, even when everything was peaceful, they told the world that they were fighting terrorists. They're very clever with the way they twist things, together with the Russians. Even the cat sanctuary has been used as part of this propaganda. We were very angry when we saw a tweet about us, posted on 15 March 2018 from the account of the Russian Embassy in Syria, using a picture of us and our sanctuary as a demonstration that 'normal life in Aleppo' had been restored (by them of course). They even used a hashtag #SyriaRestored.

But Syrians are not terrorists. They have big hearts. Throughout our history, we have hosted and welcomed people from around the world when they were refugees and were forced to flee their own countries. We've welcomed Armenians, Circassians, Lebanese, Palestinians, Sudanese and people from so many other poor countries that have suffered war and political crises. We even hosted people from Bosnia and Herzegovina in our houses. During the Kuwait war, thousands of Kuwaiti people fled to Damascus, but now Kuwait has forbidden the issuing of any visa to Syrians. Jordanians fled to Syria when they had a water crisis with Israel in the 1990s, but now Jordan won't let any Syrians across its border. Millions of Iraqis, at least 2.5 million, came to Damascus and Syria after 2003, when the United States invaded Iraq and made it unsafe to live there. So many Iraqis came and so many rich ones bought houses and property that the law had to be changed about who could buy property inside Syria, to protect Syrian rights to buy. In 2006, many Lebanese fled to Damascus to escape the war between Israel and Hezbollah. Syrians drove to the border and brought total strangers back into their homes.

Syria was the safe haven in those days. Now no one will give us a safe haven when we need it. We are sad that other Arab countries and other Arab people didn't stand with us. We didn't see any demonstrations in any Arab countries to support civilians inside Syria. We don't carry hate towards anyone. We help all people when they need us. The war has tarnished our reputation and our name. No country has welcomed us. Worse still, they've even made fun of us. We believe that all fighting parties, including the regime and the rebels, as well as all the countries who are intervening in Syria, like the United States, Russia, Turkey and Iran, are all oppressors, especially when they provided the fighting groups in Syria with a lot of weapons. They made ordinary Syrians fear that this war will never end.

I hope Idlib will not be attacked. I think, if they did, it would result in a very big, wide and expensive conflict, too expensive I hope. If the regime and the Russians do attack Idlib, it could well be even worse than Aleppo. Close to 4 million people live in Idlib Province, so where would we all go? How could Russia and the regime justify putting all the Syrian opposition in one place and then kill them all? Turkey is trying to organize the opposition groups and get them to name a single leader, so that they can then create an army and a police system to bring back law and order to the area. But at the moment everyone wants to be the leader and they can't agree on just one. There's no peace plan and no reconciliation. It's up to us to make our own reconciliation, to help each other as best we can.

Deals are already being done between groups who were enemies before. They depend on each other for things like oil and wheat. While one group has the oilfields, another has the refineries. While one group has the wheat fields, the other has the flour factories. There's a new business elite now, and the old merchant elites have been bypassed. They didn't have the networks and skills to match these new circumstances, so they've lost their positions of power. New faces are appearing on Aleppo city council, there are new Aleppo MPs in the parliament and in the Aleppo Chamber of Commerce. It's the same all over the country. They were warlords a year or two ago, but now they're accepted and considered very important. They're the new bigwigs and they've got their own mafias.

I watched an interview on television with a UN special adviser on Syria, a Norwegian man called Jan Egeland. He said he's been trying to get aid into besieged areas inside the country for years now. He said the way aid has been manipulated and made into a political football in Syria is beyond anything he has ever seen anywhere else in the world. After everything I've seen and experienced during the siege of Aleppo and afterwards, I believe him.

Part of my life came to an end on December 15, 2016,

when I had to leave my city, driving my ambulance. I was given no choice. After more than forty years, I left my city, and my home in East Aleppo, with just a small suitcase, Ernesto, and an ambulance full of wounded people. I have only my many memories left – happy and sad. Thinking of all this brings so much sorrow to my mind that I try not to remember.

Aleppo was a great city. It took thousands of years to build up through the work of hundreds of generations. It survived Mongol invasions, famines, droughts and earthquakes. But one generation has brought it down in just four years. It used to have the biggest population of any city in Syria, and more factories even than the capital Damascus, because of all the businesses that were based there. Our merchants were famous, not just the Sunni Arab ones, but the Armenian ones, the Jewish ones, the Turkmen ones, the Circassian ones, the Iranian ones and the Kurdish ones as well. We were multicultural, with lots of mosques and churches. There were synagogues too before the Jews left. There were quarrels and rivalries, of course, usually to do with money, as always in Aleppo where business is king, but on the whole we got on with each other.

People in every age have had their arguments and their wars, some worse than others. The Mongol chief Tamerlane destroyed most of Aleppo and ransacked it, killing lots of its inhabitants. He made a tower of 20,000 skulls outside the city walls before he left. After he'd gone, the Christians came back and rebuilt their community in Al-Jdaideh, which means the 'New Place'. They built it more beautiful than before. In this war, Al-Jdaideh was on the front line, heavily bombed again, but it's already being rebuilt – first the churches, then the houses. Life comes back. This regime has bombed us, committed war crimes and used chemical weapons on us, but we responded with love of life. We dream of a place where children who've been traumatized by constant bombing and war can play and learn to love animals. In the sanctuary, children have the chance to love and be loved, to trust and be trusted. I saw how much this benefited both animals and children, and this is how I learned about what a difference this kind of pet therapy could make to both children and animals – and to adults.

Most of my adventures in my life have been during the last seven years. I risked my life many times in order to help people. Before the war, work preoccupied me, but now these are the real adventures of my life. Helping people and children and animals is the perfect adventure. My life before the war does not equate to the last seven years, because my achievements of the last seven years have been far more valuable than anything I did before. I've made many friends from all around the world who've helped me in humanitarian works after they saw what I've done to help people and children. I was able to achieve my dreams and my friends have such faith in me. We hope to launch some more projects in the future. They will include a Syrian academy for children. In this academy we will try to give the children what their parents couldn't give them. We'll help orphans and non-orphans. Most of the children are poor and their parents don't have work. Children and animals are of equal importance for me, they are at the same level. I have big ambitions to help more of them in the future.

Ernesto's Sanctuary is the first of its kind in Syria and perhaps even in the whole Arab world. Arabs normally don't like animal sanctuaries and don't much like taking care of animals. Of course, if it's for business, then it's different, like for farmers who have sheep, goats and cows. They have to look after their animals otherwise their business would suffer. But in most of the Arab world, people aren't interested in animals at all. I think some people with a weak personality give vent to their weakness by hurting animals. Unfortunately, in Syria, there are no strict rules to protect animals and many people even torture them. I would say only 10 per cent of Syrians like cats. For dogs it's much less, maybe only 1 or 2 per cent. It's very rare in Syria and in Arab countries for people to have pets like cats and dogs. When I was growing up, people outside my family always thought it was strange that I liked to take care of animals so much. Only my father and my grandfather understood.

Animal welfare is the highest thing in existence, to my mind. I consider these animals are like my children. We need to feed and look after them, and I will take care of them all my life.

I find it hard to think about the future. I prefer to focus on happy moments in recent times, like planting olive and pine trees with the children at Al-Mihrab square, at the entrance of Idlib. I hope these trees remain standing for many years to come. Sometimes I worry that war will return, but only God knows what will happen. I am optimistic and try to do good things for people, in spite of all of this confusion and everything that is happening around me.

We are rebuilding our communities and my role in that is to rebuild my sanctuary for cats. Friendship between animals is a great thing and we should learn from them. I'll stay with them no matter what happens. Someone who has mercy in his heart for humans has mercy for every living thing.

I hope people will remember me after I die for the work I've done during these last seven years. I want my children to be proud of their father, to feel that he has done something good for people and the country. When they grow up, I hope they understand the reasons why I stayed behind to do this work helping these children and animals that were hurt by the war.

I do not know the moment of my death. That is not for me to decide. But I know that others after me will now continue my work. And that is enough.

Acknowledgements

DIANA DARKE

I would like to give my greatest thanks to Raida Mukarked and Ammar Hasan, two close friends, without whose help this book would not have been possible. Both are Syrian refugees displaced to Beirut from my house in Damascus by criminal war profiteers in 2014. After years submitting numerous applications for asylum in a range of countries including Britain, they were finally accepted by Human Corridors, an Italian NGO, and were about to leave Lebanon for Italy with their young family. They were euphoric at the chance to start a new life in Europe. Both are multilingual, and, before the war in Syria, Raida had been a tour guide with the Ministry of Tourism while Ammar had worked in hotel management.

Suddenly, days before their scheduled departure, Ammar's visa was rejected by Italian immigration officials. It was a case of mistaken identity – a different Ammar Hasan was on a blacklist. Immigration lawyers in Italy advised it would take at least two months to unravel the administrative paper trail and get their visas reissued. Meanwhile they were stuck in limbo in Beirut, their lives on hold, having wound down their freelance Arabic teaching and translation work in anticipation of their permanent emigration to Italy.

When the publisher was in touch with me with the idea for this book, I knew I couldn't meet the deadlines on my own and had in fact turned the offer down. But when a very distressed Raida explained what had happened to them, I realised we might be able to help each other and asked if she and Ammar would be willing to act as intermediaries with Alaa, the Cat Man of Aleppo, inside Syria. They would have to channel my questions to him, record his answers, then send me back the audios and transcripts. It would give them two months' work and much-needed income, and enable me to accept the commission.

So began a unique collaboration. Raida and Ammar were, like me, unable to meet Alaa, since he is living in opposition-held Syria. But through a mix of email, smartphone and instant messaging, they were able to pass on my messages, gradually building a relationship of trust between us all.

Throughout these two months Raida and Ammar juggled the constant interruptions of their two small children and the demands of fasting during a very hot June Ramadan, while simultaneously suffering the stress of many setbacks related to their Italian visa situation and their refugee status inside Lebanon. They had nowhere to work other than their tiny Beirut flat. But they persevered with the heavy workload and

Acknowledgements

their diligence has been exemplary. Thankfully, they also greatly enjoyed the project.

I pray that their refugee status can eventually be resolved and that they can have the new future in Italy which they so richly deserve.

Deep thanks and appreciation are also due to my editor at Headline, Fiona Crosby, who identified Alaa, the Cat Man of Aleppo, as having an inspiring real life story. Her skilful guidance and expert feedback throughout were both invaluable.

As for Alaa himself, he is a miracle of survival against the odds. One day, when circumstances permit, I hope I may even meet in person the man whose voice I have provided for this book.